Moments
In Time
Images
of Exemplary
Nursing Care

Beth Perry RN, PhD

Cover photo by Otto F. Mahler

Moments in Time
Images of Exemplary Nursing Care

ISBN 1-55119-045-1

Published by the Canadian Nurses Association, 1998.

Written by
Beth Perry RN, PhD

ACKNOWLEDGEMENT

This book is a salute to the enormous contribution that clinical nurses make to our health and well being. It is an attempt to make the often hidden but critical work of bedside nurses more visible. To you, my exemplary colleagues, thank you for telling your stories and helping us to learn to be better nurses and more sensitive individuals. I acknowledge that without your generosity this book would not have been possible.

C O N T E N T S

INTRODUCTION

THE POWER AND PROMISE OF EXEMPLARY NURSING CARE

Within most disciplines there are those who are recognized as being exceptionally competent practitioners. These people are sometimes called "expert," "unusually competent" or "extraordinary." What they have in common is that their way of working is remarkable and their actions and personal interactions are regarded by others as highly effective.

This book is based on the findings of a recent study of the beliefs, actions and interactions of a group of unusually competent oncology nurses. The investigation centred on the broad question: What is the nature of exemplary nursing practice? The nurses studied were chosen by peer nomination. These were nurses whose peers would choose to have as caregivers if they were diagnosed with cancer. Data were gathered through observation, conversation and narrative exchange. The personal accounts that appear in this book are stories as told by exemplary nurses, coupled with excerpts from field notes made during observations of their work.

Clinical nurses, nurse educators, nurse researchers and nurse administrators may find this book of value. In addition, the ideas presented here could also be meaningful to practitioners and theoreticians employed in human service fields other than nursing. The issues addressed are those basic to the experience of being human: life, death and caring. For this reason, the stories and poems that are the centrepiece of this work have potential to touch all persons.

Significance for Nurses

Clinical nurses often work in isolation. Reading about the practice of others can be a way to learn alternative approaches. The examples in this book can serve as models for beginning nurses, helping them to learn both the tangible and the less tangible components of excellent practice.

Some of the descriptions of exemplary nursing practice demonstrate how such nurses achieve their levels of competence. From these, nurse educators can draw ideas to increase the effectiveness of their teaching. There are also worthy insights for nurse educators concerned with providing continuing education for those who are already excellent practitioners.

For nurse researchers, this book poses unanswered questions. I anticipate that nurse researchers may use the descriptions, the questions raised and the insights articulated to stimulate their ideas and hypotheses for future research.

The research methodology employed is an unusual combination of qualitative methods. Nurse researchers may find this book an example of how different recognized approaches can be combined, resulting in a unique way of gathering, interpreting and presenting data.

Nurse administrators may use this book's findings in several ways. For example, it may benefit them to have descriptions of the more intangible and immeasurable aspects of nursing practice. Administrators, too, may find this useful as they attempt to define and defend the distinctive role that nursing has in the delivery of health care.

Significance for Others

In one sense, this book describes aspects of the greater search for what it means to be human. As we search for meaning in our own experience, and in the experience of others, we gain a fuller grasp of what it means to live in this world. Van Manen (1990) claims that through such an exploration we "become more fully aware of who we are" (p. 12). Those whose responsibility it is to provide service to others may find they are better able to achieve their goals if they first have a greater understanding of themselves. This work contains guidance for those who seek to become exceptional, no matter what their field of service.

The nature of nursing is such that, every day, practitioners face some of the most fundamental and poignant issues confronting humanity. Understanding the beliefs and motivations of exceptional nurses can illuminate our understanding of such issues. Ellis and Flaherty (1992) observe that "little has been done to unravel the complex manner in which emotion, cognition, and the lived body intertwine" (p. 3). I believe that this book begins to unravel the mystery.

Discovering Meanings

To come to the understandings presented, the data were analyzed in several ways. The initial analysis was made by study participants. This was provided voluntarily by nurses as they shared their narrative accounts and conversed with me.

Weaving together nurses' narratives and comments with fields notes and quotations from related literature provides additional perspectives. These elements have been arranged in themes. Such integration is consistent with a hermeneutic phenomenological approach. Poetic interpretations have also been incorporated. These poems aim to provide an expressive perspective of the narratives, comments and observations. The poems offer another – and personal – level of understanding. I hope they communicate some of the emotion of the situations they reflect.

A further perspective of exemplary nursing practice was sought through grounded theory analysis (Strauss and Corbin, 1990). Data were reviewed for additional themes and a core variable.

The final analysis is left to the reader, to form his or her own insights regarding exceptional nursing practice. Much of the data is presented verbatim, in order to facilitate this personal analysis.

In summary, two qualitative methodologies – grounded theory and hermeneutic phenomenology – were combined in the study that is the basis for this book. Each offered a unique and complementary contribution. Hermeneutic phenomenology provided the rich detail that conveys the context and humanness of the experience of exemplary nursing care, while grounded theory provided analysis at a more conceptual level. I believe that the result offers a more complete picture of exceptionally competent nursing practice than could have been accomplished by any single approach to data analysis.

Organization of this Book

In the first chapter, part of the contextual basis for the book is set. I share my most vivid memories of oncology nursing in an attempt to establish a landscape against which a description and discussion of exemplary practice can be placed. These memories also introduce myself to the reader, exposing some of my values and possible biases, allowing the reader to determine how I may have influenced what appears on these pages. A brief review of the published literature on the nature of oncology nursing and comments from some of the exceptional nurses on their views related to oncology nursing are also included.

Chapters 2, 3 and 4 each centre on a specific theme. Stories, quotations, observational accounts, relevant literature and poetic interpretations are used as illustrations. The three themes described are the dialogue of silence, mutual touch and sharing the lighter side of life.

In Chapter 5 the essence of exemplary nursing practice, joint transcendence, is described. Also discussed in this chapter is the emotional connection between patient and nurse, and affirming the value of each. Again, verbatim accounts from nurses and reflection through poetry are featured in the discussion.

Insights and implications for clinical nurses, nurse educators, nurse researchers, nurse administrators and human services workers are presented in chapter 6.

What is Nursing?

For many years, scholars have attempted to address the question: What is nursing? The question can never be fully answered, although many nursing practitioners continually search for a more complete appreciation of the question. My hope is that readers of this book will come to a better understanding of the power and promise of exemplary nursing care – and discover new perspectives on this most fundamental question of the nursing profession.

I Am Your Nurse

I am your nurse.
I ease your pain.
I bathe your skin.
I make your bed.
I rub your back.
I meet your needs.
You heal me.

I am your nurse.
I feed you meals.
I give you rest.
I tend your wounds.
I sense your suffering.
I answer your questions.
You teach me.

I am your nurse.
I know your pain.
I share your loneliness.
I feel your despair.
I taste your joy.
I sense your spirit.
You touch my soul.

And sometimes,
for just a moment,
I am you,
and you are me,
and we are one.

Together,
we go beyond the limits
of ordinary experience,
to live the extraordinary.

C H A P T E R   O N E

THE MULTI-LAYERED LANDSCAPE

There is no doubt that exemplary nursing practice is complex. Part of the complexity comes from the intricate and multi-faceted nature of the context in which nursing occurs. This context or landscape needs to be articulated in order for descriptions of exceptional nursing practice to be viewed clearly. As a preamble, a brief review of the literature on the nature of oncology nursing is presented. Statements from conversations with unusually competent nurses are highlighted in a discussion of particular aspects of cancer, the disease of primary interest to oncology nurses.

This landscape also includes a collection of my own memories – stories from my experience as an oncology nurse. By sharing these vignettes I hope to convey something of my values, beliefs and possible biases. I believe that allowing readers to incorporate an understanding of my experiences into their own will increase their general understanding of me, of oncology nursing, and ultimately of exemplary nursing practice.

Caring for People with Cancer

Nursing has been acknowledged in the literature as both a demanding and rewarding profession (Arcand, 1980; Benner and Wrubel, 1989; and Marshall, 1980). An essential feature of nursing is that it is an experience lived between human beings, primarily between patients and nurses. A therapeutic, goal-oriented process, nursing service is directed at meeting patient needs. These needs may be physical, psychological, intellectual or spiritual in nature and will differ with varying health problems.

Nurses often hold the fragility of human life in their hands as part of their everyday work life. Routinely administering complex treatments that allow for a very small margin of error can be stressful. The explosion of knowledge in health care has resulted in the increased use of technology and further complication of treatment protocols. Among the responsibilities assumed by nurses are the promotion and restoration of health, prevention of illness, attainment of a peaceful death, and maintenance of a therapeutic environment in which these goals can be achieved.

As the first line of defence and advocacy for the patient, the nurse is in a position of privilege and responsibility. This responsibility necessitates establishing and maintaining relationships with multiple professional groups. Nurses working a variety of shifts provide nursing services to patients 24 hours a day. These considerations can make nursing physically and emotionally exhausting. Fagin and Diers (1983) assert that:

> *Nursing is a metaphor for intimacy. Nurses are involved in the most private aspects of people's lives and they cannot hide behind technology or a veil of omniscience as other practitioners...in hospitals do. Nurses do for others publicly what healthier persons do for themselves behind closed doors. Nurses are there to hear secrets, especially the ones born of vulnerability [p. 117].*

Benner and Wrubel (1989) contend that those who choose to be nurses can expect frustration, despair, highs, lows and defeats often enough to remain humble. Yet, as Peplau (1952) concluded over a century earlier, nursing can be a maturing force and an educative instrument. Mallison (1987) expresses it this way:

> *If you keep working at it, learning from it...gradually you realize your palette is filling up with colors. You see more shades of meaning. You realize you are well on your way to creating a work of art, maybe even a masterpiece [p. 45].*

Oncology or cancer nursing is a specific form of medical-surgical nursing. Nurses who specialize in oncology provide nursing services to people who have cancer throughout the stages of the disease. This specialty is unique for many reasons.

First, cancer is a very common and serious disease. In 1988 it was the second leading cause of death in Canadian adults (World Almanac, 1990).

The prevalence of cancer means that most oncology nurses have had a personal association with the disease through family or friends. Some nurses have been treated for cancer themselves.

Second, the treatment of cancer is usually a lengthy process, often causing disruption in the work and family life of the patient. These disruptions, combined with the plaguing side-effects of the therapies, place demands on the patient, the patient's family and the caregivers. Highfield (1992) writes:

> *A diagnosis of cancer often provokes a crisis of meaning. Personal relationships may be burdened with an uncertain future. Formerly effective coping strategies seem inadequate...there is a rising sense of aloneness. In short, a spiritual crisis is created [p. 1].*

Third, the guilt associated with having cancer adds to the suffering of the patients and their families. Julie, one of the exemplary nurses, whose practice was studied for this book, phrased it like this:

> *Though the etiologies of many cancers are unproven, a diagnosis of cancer is often accompanied by guilt. There is a whole school of thought out there that projects to the vulnerable, grieving, cancer patient that this whole disease is their fault. Comments like, "You can fight this thing," or "With the proper attitude it can be overcome," make them feel responsible both for getting sick and for getting well. There probably is someone somewhere who drank a herbal tea, prayed in a certain position, ate peach pits, or laughed themselves into being reportedly free of cancer. But it makes the remaining millions feel abjectly guilty, as if they have done something wrong.*

Fourth, cancer is among the most culturally dreaded diseases. One of the most frightening statements a person might hear is, "You have cancer." These words bring a chill to the heart. Although some progress has been made in treating cancer, recovery can be long and painful and many people do not survive. Its chronicity and close association with death and suffering make it a somewhat taboo topic in our society. According to Benner and Wrubel (1989):

> *In society the disease cancer appears to have become the metaphor for the deepest fears held about the inevitable disintegration and decay of the body. Cancer is the disease which attacks the body organs about which greatest ambivalences are felt, those of sexuality, reproduction, and excretion. The society "battle" against cancer is then seen as the struggle to resist acceptance of the inevitability in life of death, decay, and decomposition [p. 8].*

Glaser and Strauss (1968), after extensive study of cancer care settings, conclude that the journey toward death is often more difficult for caregivers and survivors than for patients. Benner and Wrubel (1989) agree that providing nursing service for cancer patients is especially challenging because nurses need to "adopt ingenious strategies for providing comfort, nutrition, social support, rest, and activity in the midst of demanding treatment regimes and a debilitating disease" (p. 256).

Julie summarized her view of the devastating nature of cancer by the following:

> *We must realize that cancer is relentless and shows absolutely no respect for its host. Cancer writes its own rules. It teases; in fact, each remission gives a little taste of hope for normalcy. Then, there is the emotional murder of recurrence, just to reassure patients that they are at the mercy of this monster and needn't begin to think otherwise.*

My Memories

Moments in Time

> *Each of us is a collection of significant moments. If life could be distilled down to one hour in time, that hour would include a cluster of significant moments. A moment is that which recurs when needed; it is that recurrence which magnifies the significance. These moments fill our memory banks. They are our resource files, our warm fuzzies, the emotional adhesive that holds us together. They are us.*
>
> *Julie, 1993*

I believe that my own "moments in time" have a place in this book. I want to share something of myself with the reader and I feel these memories of my life as a nurse are one way to accomplish this. By including these stories I am not claiming that I am – or was – an exceptional practitioner. My purpose instead is to relate a few of my more potent memories from my experiences, thereby imparting some understanding of this world of cancer care, and of me.

The Day I Became a Nurse

She was so ill. She was bleeding to death in front of my eyes and there was little I, or anyone could do. As I helped her back to bed, her three beautiful teenage sons pressed closer to the wall and watched in horror. Not knowing how to help her, I sat down on her bed and took her hand tightly in mine. Putting aside all thoughts of the half dozen other patients who needed me, I let my energy flow into her. As silent seconds passed I felt some of her spirit pour into me. At that moment I was changed. At that moment I became a nurse.

The Bald Man with the Big Laugh

I had just been appointed chemotherapy nurse, a position I assumed with much pride and enthusiasm. The emphasis of my duties now would be on teaching the patients about the drugs they were to receive, something I really enjoyed doing.

As with any new responsibility, there was a certain amount of anxiety at first and I was shaking a little as I approached Mr. and Mrs. Zimmerman to teach them about Mr. Zimmerman's chemotherapy. However, I was determined to do well and I had a sophisticated teaching plan, complete with objectives, in hand. Sitting down, I launched into my lecture about the side effects of the drug he was to receive, the major one in his case being anticipated hair loss. At one point in my monologue, I realized that both Mr. and Mrs. Zimmerman were looking at me with some amusement. Pausing long enough to assess the situation, I realized to my embarrassment that Mr. Zimmerman was already totally bald and had been for many years as a result of natural causes. I stopped speaking, stammered a little and then we all burst into a cleansing round of laughter, laughter that swelled until the tears came.

On Melting Anger

She was such a gruff woman. My most vivid memories of her have her sitting upright in her bed issuing caustic commands to her family members and caregivers.

Being a novice nurse who was eager to please, I was succulent prey for her and she was crude, harsh and cutting in her demands of me. "Move that water jug," "fluff my pillow" and "bring me juice," she would snap. Often I was afraid to answer her call bell and face her anger. Yet as the days went on I started to like her. I looked forward to seeing her and being her nurse.

One day in response to her demand that I "help her out of bed, now," I put my arm around her shoulders to offer her support. "What are you doing?" she barked. As our eyes met I said, "I'm just trying to help you, I want you to be as comfortable as possible and I don't want you to fall and hurt yourself." She muttered a muted "Oh," but at the same time, as I held her emaciated frame tightly I felt some of her muscles relax just a little and I knew that I had touched her with my touch.

It was a Good Death

The warm amber glow of a candle filters through the quiet air. In the bed covered with a patchwork quilt that she has made a middle-aged woman breaths shallow, erratic last breaths. Her husband of a quarter century sits at her side brushing her cheeks with his stocky fingers and with occasional soft kisses. Although she is unable to talk, he tells her how much their life together has meant to him and how much he will miss her. As her breathing ceases he gives her a final kiss and turns to me. Freely, I open my arms and my heart to him in his grief. I leave them alone for a moment to say goodbye. As I go, he says, "Thank you." I smile inside, feeling privileged to have shared in the final moments of their life together.

Mama Goes to Heaven

The soft strains of music touch me as I enter her room. Around the bed, hand in hand, stand her eight children. My patient is a recently immigrated Italian woman of 60 years. Her life is nearly ended, and pain remains her greatest adversary. No amount of analgesic has soothed the relentless agony. Quietly, her family begins to work magic. As they sing softly in their native tongue my patient dozes in peace. They take turns, sometimes singing joyously in unison, other times a sweet sad solo voice is heard. As they sing she slowly slips away. They each say goodbye to their "Mama" and then move on to live the rest of their now more precious lives. After they have gone, I say my own farewell to this brave lady, and I feel honored to have helped escort her to peaceful rest.

Learning the Value of Honesty

Being so young, she quickly became everyone's favorite patient. As I enter her room she sits on her bed cross-legged, neon clad, and hugging a huge stuffed elephant. For several seconds I stare at her, struck again by the incongruence of the child-like face so clouded by the haggard expression of one who has experienced the stress of chronic terminal illness. As I sit down beside this child she looks at me and asks with penetrating frankness, "Am I going to die?" In the timeless seconds that follow my mind races, searching frantically for an answer and rejecting all the possibilities. Finally, my lips open and, as honestly and gently as I can, I say, "Yes." I know my eyes filled with tears first as we dissolved into one another's arms, grasping for the comfort of human touch. How utterly important she was to me at that moment, and how vital I was to her.

The Secret Whispers

"I miss them so much," she sighed as I washed her back and tried to make her more comfortable. "I haven't seen my kids for nearly a month. I would give anything to give them a hug." I touched her hand and as our eyes met I knew I had to help her.

Two days later it happened. Three preschoolers climbed onto their Mom's bed and blanketed her in hugs, kisses and cookie crumbs. It was such a joyous afternoon. As they leave her to return home she plants a secret whisper in each small ear, a whisper of her exclusive love for each of them.

Later that week as we struggle to save her fragile life she opens her dying eyes just long enough to tell me a secret. "Please let me go," she whispers, "I'm ready." As we withdraw the life-support equipment I am overcome with feelings of peace and achievement. We have given her the greatest gifts possible for her, secret moments with her children — and death with dignity.

Silent Music

In report they announce that I am to give one-to-one care to a young woman with leukemia. She is distressed and agitated because of recent news that her disease is no longer in remission. Knowing that I will be her constant companion for the next eight hours, I try to think carefully about the approach I will take in our conversation. What should I say? How can I let her know that what she is feeling is normal? What can I do to offer her the support I know she needs?

As I enter her room I am still unsure of my opening words, so I say nothing. Sitting close to her on her bed I take her cold hand in mine. Softly stroking her forehead I speak only with my eyes and touch. She seems relieved and I can feel the tension ease. The silence, it appears, is a welcomed friend. It feels tranquil. Nothing is frantic, nothing needs to be said. It is as if the agony and strain have been replaced by music that we can both hear.

Caring On

"Here is your patient for today." As I get off the elevator, I look up to the voice of my charge nurse. She is holding a tiny baby wrapped in a hospital blanket and she is handing the babe to me. Involuntarily, my head is shaking no, while inside I struggled to confirm what is happening. A baby – with cancer – my patient? It just can't be.

But it is true. As she transfers the wee infant to my arms, I recognize the unmistakable look of the disease etched on the little face. She is swollen from the medications and her bald head carries the bruises and scars of repeated intravenous insertions. The grey-yellow complexion of death is indisputable.

That intense encounter with the brutal injustice of cancer followed me throughout my career. Occasionally, I wonder how I kept going, how I kept caring. Much of my motivation came from a tiny pendant given to me by a friend. I wore it always. Once in a while I would catch a glimpse of it in a mirror as I gave my patients care. "Live, love, laugh," was its message. Whenever I saw it, I knew I must carry on, for my sake, for the sake of that innocent child, and for the patients I was yet to meet.

As I relive these events from my nursing years I recall that the anguish was often great. However, through these same experiences came a sense of achievement and the knowledge that I was making a difference in the lives of others. For me, cancer nursing was an incredible opportunity, a chance to be intimately involved with people who were entering one of the most critical times of their lives.

What a privilege it was to encounter the humanness of life as part of my everyday work life. I feel that I have been shaped by my experiences with cancer patients and their families. Seeing others bravely facing their disease, their treatments and their uncertain futures helped me realize how precious and precarious life is. As a result of these experiences, my life became brighter and more full of texture. Personal relationships were enriched and life took on a strange combination of urgency on one hand, and relaxed animation on the other. I was inspired to laugh liberally, cry openly, care deeply and study intently while at the same time savouring every second of each experience.

Nursing is very complex and multi-faceted. Our understanding of the actions and thoughts of those nurses who do it exceptionally well remains limited. However, I hope that describing the ways of those nurses who provide nursing care with unusual competence can enhance our awareness and appreciation of excellent practice and move us to a fuller understanding of what nursing is.

Nurse Transformed

Shaped and molded daily by
a constant stream of challenges,
you continue to evolve.

Each time you confront death,
all life becomes more treasured.

Now,
you approach life with a sense of urgency,
eagerly soaking up all of the
pleasures and pains it offers.

You want to change the world,
to make a difference in the lives of
those who need you.

But all the while
you recognize that you too must be sustained
and you receive as openly as you give.

With gratitude
you accept and welcome these changes,
and anticipate your continued transformation.

CHAPTER TWO

THE DIALOGUE OF SILENCE

Silence: pure, precise and, in a sense, perfect. There is little written about it. Silence is seldom a direct focus of research or conversation because silence is difficult to observe, record and write about.

Silence emerged repeatedly as an approach used by exemplary nurses. It is clear that nurses often used silence during emotional or difficult patient interactions. Beyond these more extraordinary times, silence also played an important part in everyday nurse-patient encounters.

Silent moments were a part of most nurse-patient exchanges. In few day-to-day human interactions is there constant, relentless verbalization. However, the silences that were part of these nurse-patient encounters were different from our average customary pauses. Most times these silences, or gaps in speech, were rich in non-verbal communication. Messages that were difficult or even impossible to speak, were sent from nurse to patient and from patient to nurse in silence. When everything that needed to be said had been said, when cultural or language barriers inhibited spoken communication, when the patient was confused, when the news was bad, when there were no "right" words, and when no words were necessary, silence was used.

There were many benefits or gifts that resulted from silence. Specifically, patients received the gift of the nurse's presence and the gift of being listened to with openness. Through providing these silent gifts, the nurses also received, making this silent dialogue beneficial to both the patient and the nurse.

It is apparent that the silence came in varying forms. For example, non-verbal messages framed in silence, silent messages encoded in words, and silent messages encoded in actions are forms of silent interplay recorded and reported in this chapter. What many of the silent moments had in common was their two-way quality. Therefore, I have called this theme the dialogue of silence.

In this chapter I combine some of the stories written by exemplary nurses with field notes from my observations and excerpts from conversations with nurses. These narratives illustrate the uses, gifts and forms of silence as well as how nurses came to learn to use silence in patient interactions.

To provide an enhanced understanding of some of these examples, a poem that I believe exposes the nucleus or heart of the narrative is presented. I consider poetry an appropriate medium of analysis because it is a bridge between non-verbal and verbal expression and it allows for communication in a succinct and creative way. Poems potentially expose the tacit – that which is difficult to express otherwise. Together, the narratives, poems and literature offer an understanding of how silence is used in exceptional nursing practice.

Learning to Use Silence

Among exemplary nurses there was agreement that "you grow into the use of silence" and that it is "a very powerful and advanced skill." These nurses confirmed that they do consciously use silence in their nursing care, but this had not always been so. Early in their nursing careers many talked about trying hard to "say the right thing" to patients and their family members. Jane, an exemplary nurse, phrased it this way: "I found that I used to worry a lot about saying the right thing. I have discovered that the 'right thing' often means saying nothing at all."

Although these exemplary nurses agreed that silence is useful and effective in conveying concern for patients and in allowing them an opportunity to express themselves, they acknowledge that it is difficult to do. Lana, an exceptional nurse, said:

> *We are a very verbal society. We talk, talk, talk. We hardly ever stop to really listen. We generally don't like silence. It is very uncomfortable, and it was for me too, especially in the beginning. It's not that you don't want to be quiet, it's just that you can't – it's not natural, at least not for me anyway.*

How did these nurses learn to practise silence effectively? They talked about observing other nurses using it with their patients. "It was just so amazing," commented Jane as she described a particular moment when a nurse she considered very capable calmed an agitated patient without a word by placing a quiet hand on his shoulder. Other nurses described how they discovered the power of silence on their own, often quite by accident. Jane told me of this experience:

> *I was with this patient I didn't know very well. His doctor just came in his room on rounds one day and said, "Your cancer has spread. There is very little else we can do for you. It doesn't look good," and left. I was blown away. Because I didn't know what to say, I just sat down on the edge of the bed and the patient and I sat there looking out the window together. I just couldn't think of a thing to say that would counter the intensity of what had been said, or make the patient feel any better. Finally, I just left.*
>
> *A few days later that patient said, "Thanks for being there when I needed you." I learned something really important from that experience.*

A Lesson Learned

There is a time to be silent,
and a time to speak.

The key is,
learning to tell the difference,
and having the temperance
to do what's right.

Part of learning to use silence is learning to recognize the different qualities of silence. Sometimes silence means that a great deal of suffering is present. Embarrassing circumstances may cause silence. Exhaustion can bring a peaceful kind of silence. Moria, an exceptionally competent nurse, talked of these differences when she commented, "I try to be tuned in to the variance in silent human sounds." Blondis and Jackson (1982) contend, "In silence people may express feelings ranging from empathy and love to resentment and hostility" (p. 18). They add, "Silence does have range, and when this is understood it becomes less threatening" (p. 18).

Times When Silence is Useful

Exceptional nurses use silence in a variety of situations; in particular when there was nothing more to be said, when communicating with patients across cultures, when their patients were dying, when their patients received bad news, when their patients were psychologically or cognitively impaired, when words were unnecessary and when there were just no "right" words. Examples of each of these applications follow.

When it has All Been Said

The Day the Words Ran Out

They have poured so freely
over the years,
like sand flowing through an hourglass.

Then one day,
like the sand,
the words just all ran out.

But don't be tempted
to turn the hourglass over,
to fill the void with endless chatter,
because no matter what you do,
the sand will never flow as smoothly again,
and we'll both just be disappointed.

Another exemplary nurse, Marie, told me the following story that illustrates this particular use of silence:

> *Joan was my patient but, more than that, we had become friends over the six years. She had come to the hospital for treatments, pain control and now for palliative care. We had shared so much: laughter, pain and true*

accomplishments. I remember how excited I felt when she was rehabilitated from major back surgery. She was able to walk again. Sure she had to use a cane, but she was travelling.... It was a miracle, and we celebrated!

Now those were only memories as she was admitted for palliative care. I enjoyed being her nurse as we shared a lot about one another's lives. She knew of my hopes, dreams and plans. I knew of her favorite things, her tears and her troubles. It was Christmas, and she was assigned to me. She struggled to speak as it now required a great deal of effort. So now, I also spoke very little. She slept and dozed off frequently as the narcotics were being increased daily. When she would open her eyes, we'd smile. I remember clutching her hand just before I left my shift and holding that grip. I wished her a beautiful Christmas; peace was my greatest hope for her.

I left the room. I remember wanting to go back to her and hesitating. Should I say "goodbye?" I didn't return. Over the years we had said a lot. The last day we said little and I still feel that was all that was needed. Silence speaks in gentler ways than words at times.

In a follow-up conversation with Marie she reflected on her story, saying,

Sometimes everything that needed to be said has already been said. If it has already been done, you have to recognize that. I had been with Joan for six years. When it came to the end there was nothing left to say. We had said it all. The words had just run out.

The Silent Parting

We have been together for a season,
and our time has been so good.
When it's time for me to go,
just place a finger to your lips
and step away.

There are no words – no adieu,
no farewell, no goodbye,
that can say anything
that we haven't already said;
that can mean any more
than you already mean to me.

When Communicating Across Cultures

In some cultures, silence is a more accepted and therefore a more appropriate means of communication. During one of our conversations, Marie recalled this memory of a young native boy she had cared for:

> *He was a young guy, a native Indian from Northern Alberta. He just didn't use many words. It wasn't his way. I knew that talking would be too much for him. It wasn't needed. When I watched his family around him, especially his Mom whom he loved very much, they just were very quiet. They just sat with him. So when I was his nurse I tried to mirror my behaviour to theirs, although I was still me. I thought that would show respect for the ground he stood on, for his culture, his ways.... You have to be able to do that and not detract from your personality and become someone you are not. It's a real art.*

Jane's story tells of a man from a different subculture of society and his silent approach to communication:

> *One elderly fellow I will always remember. He was a hermit; he lived in the mountains. Every day he would get up at 4:30 a.m. I would find him up in the lounge just sitting and smiling. The first time I saw him there I said, "You're up...why can't you sleep? Do you have pain? Would you like some warm milk? Shall I have the doctor order you a sleeping pill?" He just said politely, "No, no, no, no, I always get up early at home. You know, the birds sing their best songs in the morning."*
>
> *I just let him go with his agenda. What was I going to do, put him back to bed? He was 88 years old, and he had seen many early mornings.*

I remember him because he wasn't a man of many words. I just sat with him. We both knew darn well there weren't any birds to hear, but we just sat there listening.

I just sat with him.... We didn't talk much. I thought if I had been living alone all those years I wouldn't have much to say either. I just knew it was a great morning start for him. What I think he meant was that you do your best in the morning.

Reflective Silence

Meet my silence with silence.
Reflect my ways with your own.
See the me that I am,
not the me that you want me to be.
Sit with me
and let the silent notes of the birds' songs
sing to us.

When the Patient is Dying

Patients in the final stages of their disease are often most comfortable in an environment that provides limited stimulation, including a reduced noise level. Mindy, an exemplary nurse, confirmed this when she stated:

In the end, their cognition and ability to perceive things around them is limited, or they may become hypersensitive to the softest sound. All they need is the sense that someone is there, so just being there and touching them is the best nursing care you can give.

Dying patients often seem to appreciate silence. Silence gives patients time to evaluate what is happening and it allows them to focus without disruption. An important part of preparing to die is life-review, a reflection, an evaluation of one's life. This may be accomplished best in an environment that is quiet and free of distractions.

When the News is Bad

Throughout the course of their disease, cancer patients may receive news that is distressing. Diagnostic test results that show the tumour has returned or reports that the treatment has not been effective can be emotionally devastating. In these instances, silence was often seen by the nurses studied as the most appropriate nursing intervention.

While commenting about such situations, Jane advised, "They wouldn't understand your words, but they do understand your silence." This view was echoed by a colleague, Moria, who said, "When something is too overwhelming, silence and touch are the only things that make sense." Marie commented, "When my patients get really bad news, something that just shatters them, I just sit with them and hold them. Anything that I can think to say at a time like that won't make it better. It's just too bad to be made better."

Silent Support

Your words are lost
in a sea of confusion and pain.
They are not lifeboats for me,
they are like icebergs jamming me, ramming me,
pushing me under again, and again,
until I can't breathe.
Stop! Please stop.
Just stay with me and share my pain.

When Patients are Psychologically or Cognitively Impaired

Patients with cancer frequently have cognitive or psychological barriers that inhibit verbal communication. One field note reads:

> *Mindy has to be so skilled at alternative forms of communication. Today, none of her three patients could communicate through speech. One is deaf, one speaks only Croation, and one is heavily sedated and cognitively impaired by medication. Silent exchanges combined with*

touch were her only means of communicating important and complex
messages to each of them.

Patients who are cognitively impaired or psychologically traumatized may take longer to respond to questions or statements from the nurse. Silence invites response and gives patients time to formulate an answer. The nurses I observed were sensitive to this. Julie told me, "With sick people you have to wait, long enough to get a response.... If you are willing and able to wait you just might find out something important, but first you have to be comfortable with silence." This was supported by Jane who commented, "I use silence. It gives patients psychological space to think, to change their minds."

For patients in denial, silence is very important. This is the story of a moment observed:

> *Sitting and staring at the TV was an attractive woman, probably about*
> *30 years old, although it was hard for me to tell because she had lost all*
> *of her hair. When we entered her room, her gaze remained fixed on*
> *Oprah. The nurse walked up to her and sat down next to her. Without*
> *forcing eye contact, the nurse said, "Leigh-Ann, would you like to talk?"*
> *As the nurse sat waiting for a response, Leigh-Ann turned to her and in*
> *an angry outburst said, "There must be some mistake, it can't be me.*
> *This isn't happening. You must have the wrong person." Quickly the*
> *anger gave way to waves of sobs as the patient collapsed back into her*
> *chair. The nurse said nothing. In staying close and silent, she neither*
> *reinforced the denial nor impinged on the patient's need for it.*

Blondis and Jackson (1982) explain how silence can be used to respond to a patient in denial. They recommend that "you let your silence say, 'I am here, I will help you in any way I can. You are not alone.'" (p. 42).

When Words are Unnecessary

Nurses all described incidents in their practice where words were unnecessary. At times like these, they knew what their patients were thinking, or what they needed from them, without being told verbally. This story, written by Marie, is an example of one of these situations:

Mimi was an exotic looking Egyptian lady in her mid-twenties. A mother of three, she was a mere imprint of her former self. Mimi was suffering from the "silent killer," ovarian cancer. A bowel obstruction prevented her from eating and she was being kept alive with intravenous nutrition. No further treatments aimed at curing her disease were planned.

Her youngest child was a year old. The room was dim, as the curtains were drawn. Her children were playing in the room away in a corner. I sat on her bed as she had called and asked me to come to her. The family members brought the baby to her. Mimi turned and looked at me. "Please take her," she said, pushing the baby towards me.

At first I was puzzled by her request, but soon I knew what was happening. I eagerly took the child and held her close to me. Mimi had begun to draw away from those she loved most. She would soon begin her new journey, the end was near. Yet she wanted to see that her loved ones would still be cared for after she was gone. My accepting her baby reassured her of this in a symbolic way.

I felt very special that she called me and asked me to cradle her baby. I will always remember her. I didn't talk to her about that request. I knew what was happening, if only subconsciously. Silence was all that was needed. It gave her permission to separate, for now she was journeying alone.

Silence is Forever

Words are for now;
silence is for eternity.

When There are No Right Words

Sometimes there are no words available that will be the right words. When this happens, the nurses in the study relied on silence. This story is an example of such a situation:

Code one, one, one. My patient. My room. It was 0200 hours and staffing was minimal. My heart was pounding, adrenaline pumping. It was my patient who had arrested.

Fortunately, the cardiac response was strong and the arrest was primarily respiratory. He was in stable condition within 45 minutes of the beginning of C.P.R. I would give him one-to-one nursing care for the reminder of the night.

The next day I went to see him, as I felt I should share with him some of my thoughts during the code. I told him that I was very frightened that we might have lost him and that I was glad that he responded so well. He revealed that he was very much aware of our presence during the code.... Then he pulled out a very carefully folded letter he had written his adult son. It contained instructions that he should not be resuscitated should this happen again.

Tears dripped slowly down his cheeks as he read it to me. I listened intently, for this was a very precious "sharing" gift to me. When he finished, we enjoyed a few moments of quiet togetherness. No verbal response was needed.

Unspoken Words

The most powerful words
in the human language
may be those that are never said.

The Gifts of Silence

When a nurse is able to use silence effectively, the patients and nurses benefit in several ways. These benefits I called the gifts of silence. Two that are described in the following section are the gift of being present and the gift of listening with openness.

Being Present

The Gifts of Silence

With my silence I give you everything,
permission to cry,
to laugh,
to be silent too.

What does it mean to be present, to really be there for the patient? The literature promotes "presencing," or "being with" as one means by which nurses can assure patients they care about them. Bottorff (1991a) states: "There is something in the 'being with' that reveals the nurse's feeling with the other, regard for the other as a person, and desire for the other's well-being" (p. 244). Clayton, Murray, Horner and Grene (1991) claim that presencing is a part of establishing a connection between nurse and patient. To Watson (1989), being present is an expression of the nurse's participation in the patient's experience. Watson states that "Human presence may in some ways directly and or indirectly restore the human-centered subjectivity and dignity of both the care provider and care receiver" (p. 129).

Presencing is more than just being physically present. Marcel (1969) distinguishes between physical presence and being truly present:

> *There are some people who reveal themselves as "present," that is to say at our disposal, when we are in pain or need to confide in someone, while there are other people who do not give this feeling, however great is their good will.... The most attentive and the most conscientious listener may give me the impression of not being present; he gives me nothing, he*

cannot make room for me in himself.... The truth is that there is a way of listening which is a way of giving, and another way of listening which is a way of refusing.... Presence is something which reveals itself immediately and unmistakably in a look, a smile,...or a handshake. [p. 25-26]

For Marcel (1969), being present is communicated in part through silent measures: listening, looking, smiling and touching. As Green-Hermandez (1991) states, "Being there does not need to be verbally stated in order to be felt" (p. 120). It is more than sitting or standing beside someone, or saying, "I'm here for you;" it involves an overlapping of selves, or as Watson (1989) describes, it is a "human-to-human connectedness" where each is touched by the "human center" of the other.

The nurses I interviewed talked about being there for their patients. Jane commented:

The best way you can let your patients know you are there for them is by giving them silence. Staying with them through the silence tells them that you have time for them, that they are important to you, more important than anything else at that moment. If it's quiet, and there are no more questions and no more answers required and you still stay with them, it tells them a lot. In our culture, a lull in the conversation is a chance to leave, to physically remove yourself. If that break comes and the patient finds you still there, they know you really want to be with them.

Marie said simply, "You can really be present when you are silent."

Being present with a patient is a choice made by the caregiver. One must engage in self-discipline to gain skill in quieting and focusing one's self in order to be truly present for others. While the nurse may be concerned with fleeting time and tasks to be accomplished, the client is focused on the moment. To be effective, the nurse needs to attend to what is important to the patients, their "here and now" experience.

What does being there do for the patient? It seems that it makes patients feel emotionally and physically safe. The following field note demonstrates this:

Her patient tonight can't talk. Each breath is a struggle. He is so afraid that the next breath just won't be there. In his eyes I see an unmistakable look of panic. A laryngeal cancer and tracheostomy have taken his vocal cords and a tonsillar tumour has impaired his hearing. How can she let him know that she is there, that she cares? She doesn't say a word. As she stokes his hair, her eyes tell him what he so desperately wants to hear: that she is with him, that she will stay, that she will watch over him. Gradually, silently, he drifts off to sleep.

Bottorff (1991a) agrees with this view. She writes:

When a nurse is with us, in the sense of being present, we feel the security of her protective gaze, we feel valued as a person, the focus of her attention... We sense the nurse is close enough to feel with us, sharing the loss that accompanies the dis-ease we are experiencing in a sensitive, intimate way.... She understands. When a nurse is truly present, seeing and feeling all these things, we sense a kind of hopefulness.... For a moment, we are not alone[p. 244-245].

A story written by Julie illustrates the power of silent presence:

My first encounter with Paul was on the phone. He had heard about palliative care but wanted to clarify a few things. I could hear young children playing happily in the background. I explained about symptom management, admission criteria, etc. I thought perhaps he had an ill parent. Who knows, maybe he was a reporter, a philanthropist, or maybe he wanted to volunteer? His questions were well-prepared and specific. The closest I could get to asking, "Why do you want to know this anyway?" without feeling I had intruded, was saying, "We are here to help. Please feel free to call back if we can be of any further assistance."

Some weeks later a Paul was admitted to room 6. The door was always shut, his wife and his two children visited daily. He was waiting to die. He withdrew from everyone.

I could almost guarantee that when I was on he would be part of my assignment as the other nurses find this kind of patient frustrating. It seems no matter what you give, nothing comes back.

Finally, one day in sheer desperation, I heard myself saying, "Paul, this is Julie your nurse. Yes, I'm your nurse again today. And I know this isn't fair but you're just going to have to put up with me. You see I am your nurse and you deserve just as much time as any of my other patients."

As the scenario evolved, I spent time with him. Sometimes I would read to him, mostly we would just be together.

In one way, he was still waiting for the promised miracle. One day we did discuss the whole thing of miracles. Yes, there was a miracle there; it wasn't the one he had hoped for, but it was there nevertheless. We celebrated his daughter's fourth and son's first birthday on the unit. It was clear as the days passed that this little boy was his Dad's miracle. The spitting physical image of his Dad, he learned to walk in our long hallway. Both kids and Dad would take over our hot tub with mountains and mountains of bubbles (Yes, they do plug the jets and you have to call maintenance to fix it!). You see, that little boy was conceived after Paul's diagnosis and was born with the astrological sign of Cancer. The odds said that Paul should have never seen his child born, never mind walk, say "Daddy," or demonstrate his Dad's incredible shyness.

Paul continued to be "my patient." The door was still closed most of the time and we still spent a lot of our time together without exchanging many words. But one day, I will never forget as long as I have the privilege of living. I opened his door, not really knowing what I was going to encounter that day, to see him lying there with a single yellow rose in his hand and a card that said, "For Julie." We didn't say anything, we just hugged. I came out of that room and totally lost it. I don't usually hesitate to share tears with my patients, but for some reason, that day, I really lost it. The sheer intensity of that moment, even as I write it down, still makes me cry.

Breaking Through

Words, words, words,
jackhammers pounding
against my protective wall of isolation.

They do not crack it.

Gentle, silent presence
passes through the wall,
and dismantles it,
without even leaving a mess.

Listening with Openness

Silence is important for listening and for hearing the message. You must be silent if you wish to listen to another person, to listen with openness. Listening with openness involves silencing not only your voice, but also your mind. Only if you are silent in these ways can you receive and give the gift of listening with openness.

An exemplary nurse named Maureen said, "Good listening is an essential ingredient for providing nursing care of good quality." She went on to say, "Listening, listening is the biggest part of nursing. You need to be an active listener. The best nurses are the best listeners." Maureen then recalled a specific incident when, she believes, that really listening was all a patient needed from her:

Dani was a 32-year-old woman who should have had the rest of her life ahead of her. She was married and had two young children, one four, and one six months old. During her most recent pregnancy she had noticed a change in a mole above her right eye. The surgical removal of the mole had been unsuccessful and the wide-spread metastases were diagnosed quickly after that. She developed a cord compression which didn't respond to radiation therapy, so she could no longer walk.

This particular incident occurred during her final admission. I was working nights and I had just finished my 0300 hour round. I entered Dani's room to find her wide awake staring out the window. I walked up to her and asked if she was having trouble sleeping. She said that she had been lying awake thinking about life and what she had accomplished. I asked her if she would like me to stay and sit with her awhile. She accepted, telling me how frightening nights could be. I put down her side-rail and pulled up a nearby chair. I laid my hand on top of hers and for an hour I sat and listened to her. She told me how she had met her husband, about her university years, her brief career, her adventure in Europe, and finally about her two children. Her biggest regret was that she wouldn't be able to see them grow up. After she shared this with me she seemed to relax. I started gently stroking her forehead and she finally slept.

Listening with Openness

As I listen to you speak,
my ears catch the sound,
but my heart absorbs the message,
and I allow myself to be changed by your words.

In this way,
listening is a gift to you,
but it is equally a gift to me.

A common way we communicate understanding is by listening, not passively but actively, letting people know they are being attended to, heard and understood. Nurses have to be able to let their patients know that both the factual and the emotional content of what was communicated have been heard. This kind of listening actively seeks the other's feelings. Succinctly stated, effective listeners are people who use silence with as much eagerness as they use talk.

One way to accomplish this is by asking questions that encourage the patient to continue or elaborate and then remaining quiet while they answer fully. The silence indicates compassion, acceptance and support, as well as a willingness to be part of the patient's experience.

O'Banion and O' Connell (1970) provide a sensitive account of listening with openness:

> *All of me that I am in touch with and can command is directed toward you, what you are saying. All the facets of my being that feel are ready to receive your feelings. I begin to feel the struggle of your wanting to share with me; not being me, not trusting me, not knowing if I understand what it is you want to share. I feel your struggle and offer support. I want to understand. I know this is not easy for you. I lean toward you, I am ready to hear and feel, I am to be trusted. You share more, I do not retreat. I seem to want to understand. I seem to know what you are feeling. The pain grows strong and the tears relieve the pressure inside. I do not run away, I move closer, I touch a tear and say, "What do these mean?" Your pain touches the feeling of my pain and I respond with like pain. We share tears. I care for you [p. 161].*

The Difference

When I hear – I hear.
When I listen – I feel.
I make room in myself for you.

Forms of Silence

In observing nurses it was possible to identify several different forms of silence, specifically, non-verbal messages framed in silence, silent messages encoded in words, and silent messages encoded in actions. Each of these forms is described in turn in the following paragraphs.

Non-Verbal Messages Framed in Silence

Blondis and Jackson (1982) contend that non-verbal communication is a "two-way mime performed on the stage of the unconscious conveying messages that are only partially transmitted verbally" (p. viii). Non-verbal behaviour is a code that is impossible to fully describe, yet it is understood by all.

Kagen, Evans and Kay (1986) provide a more unambiguous definition of non-verbal behaviour, suggesting that it is "anything about social performance that is not speech" (p. 44). This can include gestures and movements, facial expressions, proximity, touch, self-touching, gaze, posture, gait, dress, accessories and emblems (p. 48). These researchers specify that some non-verbal responses such as close proximity, prolonged eye contact, touch and a calm, soothing voice can reassure the patient.

During my time in the nursing unit, I made the observation that non-verbal gestures may be accompanied by words but that the real message that is being communicated non-verbally is almost always framed in silence. The nurses seemed aware of this and trusted the silent non-verbal messages above their patients' verbal responses.

The following is a moment I observed. The nurse in this case, Julie, was sensitive to the non-verbal message being sent by the patient's mother. Although the message was subtle and could have been easily misinterpreted or ignored, the nurse recognized it as a significant moment and captured the opportunity to help this mother:

> *The mom of an 18-year-old girl with a brain tumour was standing outside her daughter's room, staring at the coffee maker, fumbling with her cup and apparently about to pour herself a coffee. The nurse I was observing, Julie, walked up to her and said, "You need a hug." She gave the mom an extended bear hug and without further words guided her to a private corner of the unit where they sat and talked.*

> *Her daughter, the patient, had just told her mother that when she died she would go to heaven and be a star shining down on everyone. This image had been too much for the woman to bear. After Julie talked to the mom she was able to go back into the room and be with her daughter.*

When I asked Julie about this encounter, she said, "Didn't you see the look in her eyes, and the way she was standing. She didn't want any coffee – she just couldn't bring herself to go back in the room. I could just tell she was ready to break." Julie had detected the non-verbal message framed in this family member's silence.

Silent Messages Encoded in Words

There were times during my observations when I saw the nurse's seek, find and decode silent messages, requests and pleas from the patients that were encoded in words that, on the surface, carried a completely different meaning. The delivery of high quality care depends on understanding patient's needs, many of which are expressed indirectly.

On one occasion a patient rang her bell and, as we entered the room, the distressed woman said, "The baby won't settle and needs a little pat. Bring the baby here and I will give him a rub." As I looked around the room for a non-existent baby, the nurse, after pausing for a moment, turned the patient onto her side and gave her a back-rub. Leaving a very content patient the nurse said to me, "I understood what she meant. She just needed a little attention herself." This same patient had been labelled as "confused" by some other staff members.

Sharp, accurate perception is a necessary ingredient of meaningful patient care. An exceptional nurse is discerning, knows the patients well, and is able to anticipate their needs by reading the silent messages in their words. For example, Julie told me:

What the patients say isn't always what they mean. Yesterday, I offered a patient a back rub. She said, "No, I'm OK." I just knew that she didn't want to say no. She really would have liked to say yes, but she didn't want to bother me or take any of my time. So I said, "Of course you are OK, but how about a treat?" A big smile came across her face and I gave her the rub. We both felt good about it.

Hologram of Life

Hidden in our everyday conversations,
are the things we would like to say
if we only had the courage.

Many messages need to be communicated between nurse and patient. In an environment that is frequently emotionally laden, some of these messages are difficult to say. As a result, encoding messages in safe words occurs. This is an indirect way of saying what needs to be said. It happens in conversation initiated by either the nurse of the patient. For example, Mindy called the son of a patient whose condition had deteriorated and said, "Your Dad's not able to be up at all today. He can't recognize any of us and his breathing is poor." Translated this means, "Your Dad's probably dying. Please come quickly." I asked Mindy about this conversation and she explained it this way:

> In a situation like this, I usually try the gentle approach at first. If it doesn't work, if they just don't get it, I become as direct as I need to be to get my patient's needs met. I think the more subtle angle is good because it gives the person you are talking to a chance to come to the sad realization on their own. It's not forced on them. It's not so harsh, it's just more human somehow. But it is still honest, not just as directly honest.

The following is Jane's story about a patient's encoded message for her:

> It had been a very long day. I had six patients, all requiring complete care so I was really tired. Mrs. Marshall was particularly time-consuming. She had cancer of the cervix that had spread throughout her abdomen. The draining fistulas around her groin area necessitated frequent dressing and linen changes. It was close to the end of my shift and as I changed her bed and tucked her in I managed a quick "bye" and hurried out of the room, anxious to go home. She called after me, "Thank you Jane. Take care of yourself." I replied, "OK, I will," and rushed down the hallway.
>
> After I'd taken about 20 steps I stopped. Something was wrong. It wasn't what she had said, it was how she said it. Mrs. Marshall was trying to tell me something.
>
> I went back to her side, took her hand and said, "You're saying good bye, aren't you." She said that she knew her death was near and that she wouldn't see me again but she wanted me to know how much my

care had meant to her. I thanked her too for all that she had taught me about life and death. Then we said a proper goodbye.

The next morning when I went to her room it was empty. I would have been so sad if I hadn't heard her message.

Hide-and-Seek

Like children in the garden,
we play hide-and-seek with our words.
I hide, you seek.
You seek, I hide.
Back and forth we go.

Why do we play this game?
We really have no choice.
We need a cushion, a cloud around our words.
It keeps them from bumping into our emotions,
and breaking them to bits.

Silent Messages Encoded in Actions

Mindy recounted situations in which she believed her actions transmitted powerful messages to her patients and the family members. In Mindy's estimation, silent messages can be encoded in nursing actions that communicate meaning more adequately than words can. Mindy said:

> *Sometimes what the nurse does and how she does it communicates so much to the patient and family. When a patient is close to death for example, the family focuses on the small physical things like uncut toenails, uncombed hair or wax in the ears. I make sure these things are all taken care of. It doesn't do much for the patient, but it reassures the family that all that can be done is being done and that I care about the patient.*

In our conversations nurses often referred to the importance of how they perform their work. They talked about being confident in their actions, meeting the patient's needs quickly, keeping the work environment neat and keeping "inappropriate" staff behaviour out of the sight of patients. The major reason for this concern about how the care is delivered is summed up in Lana's comment:

The patients and their families are always watching us. They determine how good we are, by how we do things. How you do your work tells them a lot. They don't know if you are doing a procedure correctly or not, but they do know if you are working confidently. We want them to have confidence in us. We have to show them by how we meet their needs that they can trust us. That they matter to us.

Another exemplary nurse, Peter, said:

Doing the little things like folding their pyjamas and putting them away in the morning, remembering to warm up their milk if they like it that way, bringing them two different flavours of jam to choose from...it might seem trivial, but it is critical.

This field note describes a scene that was an example of Peter and his colleague being mindful of the small details in their care and the message this communicates:

The patient is a very elderly Oriental lady. She is unable to speak or understand English. Today she is dying. They tend to her often, making sure she is comfortable. They select the prettiest nightgown from the hospital collection, a blue flowered one that complements her complexion. They choose one with long sleeves (because she is always cold). Every time they turn her, her hair is combed, her mouth and eyes are moistened. She is too weak to drink from a straw, so a few droplets of water are gently placed on her tongue. All of these actions are done with such gentleness. Their hands don't make a sound as they move from task to task.

During a conversation Marie made this comment:

> *I try to make my patients feel like they are the most important people in the world to me for the moments that I am with them. That has been my goal. It's the little things that make a patient feel important, like the way you enter a room is important. I consciously slow down my pace as I go through their doorway. I attend to their needs in short order, not waiting to be reminded. If I can, I anticipate their wants, like an extra pillow or a glass of juice. It makes a big difference to them. What I do and how I do it tells them so much.*

Julie talked about the importance of another silent action, keeping promises made to the patients:

> *I try to always keep promises. If I say I'll be by to make their bed at 1000 hours, then I'm there at 1000 hours, not five minutes after. If I get busy, I stop by and tell them I will be delayed... It tells them that they are important to me.*

In all of these examples, the nurses are transmitting silent messages to the patients, messages that are encoded in their actions. The nurse's actions are observable by the patients, and their interpretation of these actions may affect the nurse-patient relationship in many ways.

Because nursing work involves two-way communication, patients also transmit silent message in their actions. Mindy told me this story about an elderly Russian gentleman:

> *He couldn't speak a word of English. I had just finished making him a cup of tea because he loved tea with breakfast and the kitchen staff always sent him coffee. When I brought him his cup he didn't say anything, he just reached right up and kissed me.*

The Kiss

When you meet my needs
you tell me that you care for me.
That even though I'm old and sick
I still have value,
I still have worth.
I kiss you.
It's the only way I have to say
I treasure what you do for me.
You keep me whole.

This example, like many of the others in this chapter, illustrates the two-way nature of silent communication. Silence is used by both the patients and the nurses during their encounters. In this way it is a dialogue of silence.

Reflections on the Dialogue of Silence

As a reflective summary, each of the qualities of silence suggested in the opening sentence of this chapter – purity, precision and perfection – are discussed in the following sections.

The Purity of Silence

Words are often not what they seem and are sometimes used to camouflage what is actually felt. From observations and interviews, as well as my past experience, it appears that silence provides the purest form of communication.

Wordless messages are not likely to be interpreted in any way by the sender before they are sent. When we use words to communicate, we are in a sense often analyzing our own thoughts before sending them. To put a feeling into words, we usually first think of what we are trying to say and then of how it can be phrased. We may decide to couch or limit the expression of our true emotions, needs or thoughts by the words we choose. When we send a message in silence however, it is uncontaminated by words that are open to misinterpretation by the receiver or limitation by the sender.

Silence does not have to be used alone. It is often combined with other non-verbal and verbal forms of communication. Doing so does not diminish its purity. Sometimes this increases its effectiveness, such as when silence is combined with appropriate touch. At other times silence is best left unadulterated and untreated – just whole and real.

Silence is Precise

If we were to depend on words alone to communicate our needs, fears, hopes and feelings, not only would our communication be susceptible to inaccuracies, it would be slow. Words are often not efficient; they can be imprecise and awkward. It frequently takes many words to convey a single emotion and, when one's feelings are put into words, they can be misinterpreted.

Alternately, a silent moment can convey a myriad of emotions, precisely, quickly and accurately. Jane, in analyzing a narrative she had written said, "Silence is more filled with communication than words can ever be."

Not only are words often inadequate and lacking in precision, they can be destructive to the nurse-patient relationship. Phrases such as "It will be OK," "I know how you feel" and "Don't worry" are not only ineffective, they can convey a message that is the antithesis of what the words are meant to say. When we were discussing this notion, Moria commented:

> When I'm tempted to say something like "You'll be fine," an alarm goes off in my head and I just shut up. Saying, "You'll be fine" is like saying, "I really don't care about you or your situation. I'm uncomfortable with you sharing your feelings with me. I don't know how to answer you. Please stop talking." It doesn't do the patient any good at all. You are much better off saying nothing.

Sharpened Words

Words between us are few.
But the words we do share,
these words are like arrows,
sharpened by the silence.

Blondis and Jackson (1982) provide a succinct summary of how a nurse's actions without words can communicate with great precision:

It does not take a lot of words to tell the patient you really care. You tell them best by going directly to them as you enter the room, staying close to them, physically touching them, and asking them with your eyes what their needs are [p. 170].

Silence is Perfect

Silence is a vessel for carrying messages. It is limitless in capacity and nearly always free of defects. In silent messages there is little of the message lost. The silent meaning goes by a direct route – from the mind of the sender to the mind of the receiver. It is not filtered first through a mesh of imprecise words. Although non-verbal gestures can be deliberately pre formed and are open to misinterpretation, silence is largely exempt from these frailties. Silence takes non-verbal communication to a higher level of interpersonal exchange.

Silence is especially effective for transmitting feelings and emotions – things for which we do not have words. Compassion, acceptance and support are communicated best by silence. In an emotionally laden environment, these communications are frequently necessary and often the words we have available are too limited to communicate such subtle and intense meanings and messages.

When silence is used constructively, the nurses can have stronger ties with their patients. Physiologically, psychologically and spiritually, there are times when patients need silence. If the nurses can recognize these times, they can be very effective caregivers. Silence gives patients, their families and nurses what they are often lacking in the very public environment of a hospital: privacy and psychological space.

In silent moments, the spirits of both the patient and the nurse can be nurtured. Perhaps perfect silence can be the ultimate encounter between nurse and patient; as Watson (1989) suggests, it can be an opportunity for the restoration of the human dignity of both the careprovider and the patient.

Taylor (1991) writes, "Silence is not void, but productive...silence rings" (p. 353). Caputo (1978), in like vein, asserts that to "hear what is spoken in silence all voices and sounds must be put away and a pure stillness must be there, a still silence" (p. 117).

Such silence is crisp, clear and pristine. Creating a space where stillness can be found provides an atmosphere were patients are listened to and understood, where messages are sent and received unblemished by the static of the airways. For this to happen, the nurse must have the self-discipline, combined with awareness of self and situation, to remain appropriately silent.

Jane shared this story of her discovery of the impeccability of silence:

> *It was such a cold February day. My patient had just died. The family hadn't made it in time. I felt so sorry that I did not call them sooner. As they arrived on the elevator, I greeted them without words and took them to the bedside. We stood huddled together in silence. I remember thinking at the time, "My God, it's so quiet. This is so good. This is just what we need." In the privacy of our own thoughts, we were each able to come to a realization of the meaning of the loss for each of us.*

Perfect Silence

Someday,

after we understand
the genetic code of all life-forms,
the components of all universes,
the intricacies of all human interactions,
we will understand and use silence.

Then,

for the second time
in the history of the human race,
we will have learned to fly.

C H A P T E R   T H R E E

M U T U A L   T O U C H

This chapter develops the theme of mutual touch using field notes and the words of the exceptionally competent nurses. Again, poems combined with narrative comments are featured.

Included in this chapter is a definition of mutual touch, as is a discussion of the importance of touch in health care is elaborated to provide some context for descriptions of eight types of touch observed. Specifically, the eight types of touch used by the exemplary nurses are: procedural touch, non-physical touch, talking touch, trigger touch, social touch, diagnostic touch, comforting touch and the final touch.

The nature of touch is examined under the following headings: what is touch, touch in our society, touch and culture, qualities of touch, the language of touch and touch used with other mediums of communication. Reference is made throughout the chapter to literature on the utilization of touch in effective nursing care.

Mutual Touch Defined

The second theme I call mutual touch. Touch by its nature is reciprocal, it affects both the person initiating the touch and the person being touched. It is impossible to touch someone without also being touched yourself, therefore touch is a shared activity. As this opening poem suggests, perhaps both the nurse and the patient are affected when a touch occurs.

The Hug

Arms entwined.
Warmth exchanged.
Heart beats felt.
Concern sensed.
Care given.
Care given.

Early in my observations of exceptionally competent nurses, it became evident that touch was important in the care given. These careproviders used every opportunity to touch their patients in a spectrum of ways in order to accomplish a variety of purposes. One field note reads:

She often sits on the bed next to her patients, or she stands very close to their chairs. This physical closeness seems to create an air of familiarity. It makes their relationship close very quickly. With these nurses and their patients there is a sense of urgency.... They seem to be saying, "We might not have too long, let's cut through the formalities, let's not play games, let's invite each other in right away." Touch seems to be one way they make this connection.

After another day in the unit I recorded this observation related to the use of touch:

It was by touching, by holding her hand, laying a cold cloth on her forehead, and rubbing her sore back, that the nurse communicated that she cared. All that she did with touch said how much she wanted to help.

The Importance of Touch in Health Care

Naisbitt (1982) writes, "We must learn to balance the material wonders of technology with the spiritual demands of our human nature," (p. 40) because "when high tech and high touch are out of balance, dissonance results" (p. 44). Tough (1989), in agreement with this point of view, adds, "Beyond technology nurses have much to offer patients, they can offer themselves as well as their hands" (p. 120).

Upon entering a hospital, people encounter an unfamiliar, aseptic environment. White-coat – clad caregivers move swiftly about the maze of corridors. Steel-wheeled chairs and stretchers clatter, and machines flash and beep. The alien odour of antiseptic solution drenches the air. Hospitalization is a frightening, disorienting and depersonalizing experience.

In such an environment, Watson (1989) points out, "The care-giver provides a human presence that touches another's mind or spirit" (p. 130). Human touch becomes imperative. It restores the human element, telling patients in a concrete way there are caring people here. Touch can reach past the bureaucratic-technological system and scientific treatment, allowing the patient to reach out of the solitude of suffering.

While in hospital, a patient's psychological well-being is threatened. There is depersonalization and sensory deprivation. The effect is anxiety-provoking. Gadow (1984) adds that anxiety is among the most common and strongest responses to hospitalization. This point is also made by Sims (1986), who explains that anxiety associated with the stress of hospitalization must be countered by intervention involving caring, touch and human contact.

One branch of the healing community that has recognized the importance of touch is nursing. Montagu (1986) attributes the use of touch by nurses to two conditions. First, the majority of nurses are women and, second, nursing tasks often require that nurses are in close physical proximity to their patients. He concludes that nurses have been in a far better position to appreciate the importance of touching in the care of the patient and therefore it has become a natural part of nursing. In agreement with Montagu, Bottorff (1991b) contends that touch is universal and basic to the nurse-patient relationship.

One of my field notes describes the liberal use of touch by an exceptional nurse:

> *The use of touch is very evident. On entering the room of almost every patient, the nurse takes the patient's hand, or places a hand on their shoulder. The nurse almost always go the patient's face, instead of addressing a patient from the foot of the bed or the doorway. Standing close, making physical contact and talking directly to their patient is the most common position these nurses take.*

Marie said, "Nursing is wonderful because you get to touch the patient." Another nurse Jane states, "Touch is a part that nurses provide in a different way than other caregivers. Doctors touch the patients because they have to. We touch the patients because we choose to."

The nature of the nurse-patient relationship is such that touching is both inescapable and acceptable. Touch is the most personal of our senses because it brings two human beings into physical contact. To carry out nursing procedures the nurse must move into the patient's personal space. Blondis and Jackson (1982) explain that everyone has this personal space "an invisible area that surrounds their body" (p. 17). This space, they claim, is dynamic and varies from person to person. Only by decreasing the physical distance and crossing into this area are the touching behaviours, such as holding, hugging, grasping and stroking, possible. The physical space of both the patient and the nurse overlap when one touches the other.

Although it is understood that nurses move into the patient's physical space to provide care, the nurse must also be willing to accommodate the patients in their own space. For it to be a meaningful touch, in which messages are communicated and received, there is usually unspoken agreement that they are both willing for this encounter to occur.

Nurses have implicit permission to touch patients because of their role. Benner (1984) emphasizes the unique role of nurses in that "By their very position, nurses are asked different questions and looked to for different kinds of help than other professionals" (p. 165). Julie expresses a similar view. She said, "Nursing invites you into places you would never go, across the barriers to people, holding their hands and being close."

Nurses' comments and stories reflected a belief in the importance of touch in nursing care. Jane states, "Touching is critical. Empathy, caring, love, and concern are all transferred through your eyes and hands." Lana emphatically proclaimed, "Touching...I think it is necessary. I think it is mandatory." After a particularly demanding day, Moria commented, "I like to leave a bit of myself behind for my patients. I do that with my touches.... I hope that the feeling of being safe and cared about that I communicate to them with my touch lingers on after I have gone. I believe that it does." Still another nurse, Mindy, confided, "I have had a really good day when I have made a connection with a patient...feeling comfortable sitting on their bed or giving them a hug, touching them in some way."

The Nature of Touch

In the following sections, various aspects of touch are addressed in an attempt to bring the reader to a greater understanding of the nature of touch. Specific mention is made of the use of touch in our society, the culture-specific influences on the use of touch, the qualities of touch, the language of touch and the potential in combining touch with other mediums of communication.

What is Touch?

Touch is a powerful, sometimes disregarded, and always complex channel of interpersonal communication. McCorkle and Hollenback (1985) describe touching as a therapeutic event. They add, "It is not as simple as a mechanical procedure or a drug, because it is, above all, an act of communication" (p. 85). Watson (1985) contends that touch causes the dissolution of boundaries between two persons (p. 129). It is described by Tough (1989) as a conductor of messages, and by Montagu (1986) as capable of "soothing ruffled feelings, assuaging pain, relieving distress, giving reassurance and making all the difference in the world" (p. 282).

Benner (1984) goes further, describing touch as a conveyer of "messages as well as physical stimulation and comfort" (p. 64). She emphasizes that touch signifies an emotional involvement on the part of the nurse, a concern or caring for another. Watson (1985) agrees, saying, "Touch is concern made tangible...an expression of the nurse's participation in the patient's experience" (p. 129).

We struggle with putting into words that which seemingly lies beyond words. Because of this sense of helplessness with the language we turn to touch, the silent communication. Montagu (1986) supports this assessment adding that "Touch is always individualized, the interpersonal communications effected through touch will tend to be significant in a way that verbal language cannot achieve" (p. 133).

Referring to the shared nature of touch, Montagu (1986) writes, "Touch differs from all other senses in that it always involves the presence, at once and inseparable, of the body we touch and our body with which we touch it" (p. 125). Touch is automatically reciprocal. A nurse cannot touch a patient without also being touched. In this way the nurse and patient share the experience. Touch is a way to reassure another person that you are present in the fullest sense of the word.

Exemplary nurses, when discussing their touching behaviours, emphasized the importance of touch being genuine to be effective, to achieve this sense of being there for the patient. They said:

> *The touching has to develop in time. When I touch someone or embrace them it has to be real for me too.*
>
> *It needs to be real. If it's phony, forget it.*
>
> *It can't be forced. You have to be comfortable with it yourself first.*

Touch in Society Today

Although there is agreement that touch is an important interpersonal method of communication, fundamentally necessary for development and maintenance of health, Montagu (1986) explains that it is increasingly being denied many people. In his words, "Cuddling, caressing, embracing, stroking, the basic human touches, are withheld from the majority of people in our society" (p. 133).

When a person is sick, disfigured and deformed from cancer and cancer treatments, the withdrawal of human contact would seem even more likely. Withdrawal happens at a time when the benefits of touch are critically needed. Jane observed, "The elderly and dying especially hunger to be touched. Many of my patients, when I offer them my hand, clasp it so tightly, like it is a life line or some treasure they are guarding. Sometimes they even reach for me before I reach for them." Mindy said, "Touch seems especially important for the elderly patients.... Their hearing and vision are not good and they are often starving for touch." Bartenieff and Lewis (1980) support these observations. They explain, "In the aged and chronically ill especially, the need for tactile stimulation is a hunger which often remains unsatisfied" (p. 292).

Touch and Culture

Montagu (1986) cautions that a wide range of class and cultural differences in attitudes and practices related to tactile behavior exists. The nurses studied were cognizant of these cultural variances and respected their patients' beliefs and preferences.

During a conversation Marie remarked, "I am quite reserved about touch initially. I stand back at first and see what dance they want to dance. I think it's just good nursing to assess it. Not all the same approaches work for every patient or every nurse."

McCorkle (1974) provides a fitting conclusion, emphasizing that patients from varying backgrounds may differ in "both the manner in which they express the need for tactile stimulation and the manner in which they satisfy it...but the need is universal and is everywhere the same" (p. 126). To be truly beneficial, it is apparent that tactile communication must be used appropriately, taking cultural mores into consideration.

The Qualities of Touch

The qualities of touch can vary. To be effective in patient care situations, certain elements of touch are most desirable. For example, caring is transmitted through touching that is neither rushed nor rough in quality.

Bartenieff and Lewis (1980) detail three different qualities of touch: the fleeting light poke, the constrictive two-dimensional grip and the three-dimensional enveloping hold. They describe the three-dimensional touch as slightly "bound in nature" and explain that it communicates reassurance and support to the patient. In their opinion, this non-linear, total touch is the most effective in nurse-patient relationships: "A profunctional peck on the cheek is no substitute for a warm embrace, nor is a conventional handshake capable of replacing a caressing hand" (p. 396).

The nurses interviewed also identified different qualities of their touches. Being mindful of the importance of individualizing their care, the nurses suggested that they were careful to use touches with which their patients felt comfortable. Marie commented:

The last thing I want to do is scare one of my patients or their families members off because they feel smothered by my physical attention. I try to fit the approach to the patient. Sometimes it's hard to tell with people. If you just talk to them they may seem reserved and not very demonstrative. But if you do take the risk and give them a little test hug, they usually cling on very tightly.

It is difficult to determine some qualities of a touch from a distance. As an observer, the amount of pressure, whether hard or soft, light or heavy; and the temperature, whether warm or cold, of touches could not be determined. It was possible to see however, that the touches used by the exceptionally competent nurses were gentle, not rough, and deliberate and slow rather than rushed. This moment observed provided an example:

"What can I do to help you sleep better on your first night with us?" the nurse asks a newly admitted patient. The patient, a very frail cachexic man, is withdrawn and reserved. He says nothing.

Not giving up, the nurse makes suggestions. "How about a back-rub or a foot-rub?" She watches the patient for a clue, and when he smiles slightly at the mention of a foot-rub they set a mutually agreeable time for it to occur.

It is one of the most genuine messages of caring I can imagine. The lights are dimmed, the lotion warmed, her voice is soft and often silent. She stands at the foot of his bed so she can look at him as she does her work. Although her night is hectic, she takes her time, moving slowly and lovingly. When she is finished she wraps his feet in warmed towels to prolong the physical and psychological effects after she is gone. The message that he is still an important and worthy person, and that she cares for him, is clearly communicated through her touch.

You Have the Touch

The touch.
Soft,
gentle,
deliberate,
warm.

The Language of Touch

In the literature, touch has been described as a language. Montagu (1986) suggests it is the language of the senses. Tactile symbols create the language of touch, producing a channel of communication. Different qualities of touch used in various combinations are like the phrases of the language. Messages are communicated through this channel. The repetitive nature of touch is like the repetition of words in the language. Repetition in touch adds emphasis the same way that repetition in spoken language does.

Repetitive Touch

I move my hand over yours,
over and over and over.
I don't want to just say,
"I am here for you."
I want to say it very loudly.

The language of touch can communicate affection and warmth (Bartenieff & Lewis, 1980), acceptance and support (Blondis & Jackson, 1982), caring (Watson, 1989) and it can reassure (Montagu, 1986). Like other languages, exceptional nurses believe the language of touch can be learned. Many spoke of learning it through experience. Marie noted:

In the beginning I never touched my patients except to perform care. It took me a long time to get comfortable with it – it took me a long time to learn to look past what I was seeing in the bed and see the real person lying there and to feel all right about touching them. Part of it was experience, life experience and nursing experience. Maybe part of it too is just being more comfortable with yourself and the situation.

Touch Combined with other Mediums of Communication

Touch is seldom used in isolation, as the sole means of communicating with a patient. Regularly, as nurses touch their patients, and their patients touch them, they also engage in other verbal or non-verbal interactions. Most commonly, silence and eye contact were combined with touch.

Touch and silence

Touch and silence are often combined: although touch may be accompanied by words, it is frequently more meaningful without them. There are times when the best expressions of empathy and concern are in non-verbal touch. The following is an example of how touch and silence were combined to provide support for a family member:

> *Her husband of many years has just died from his cancer. She has been out of the room making calls to relatives as the nurse tidies up the patient's room and prepares the body. The wife enters the room and approaching the nurse says, "How can I thank you?" and begins to cry. The nurse embraces her in a tight enfolding hug. For a few minutes the wife sobs softly into the nurse's shoulder. As she cries, the nurse continues the hug. When the crying stops, the nurse gently releases her and wipes her tears with a tissue that has been waiting in her pocket for just such a crisis. Maintaining contact with the wife by keeping her arm around her shoulder, the nurse walks the woman to the elevator. No words are ever spoken. No words are needed.*

Magnified Touch

Silence,
a magnifying glass
for touch.

Touch and eye contact

Blondis and Jackson (1982) declare that the emotional truth is expressed non-verbally. Montagu (1986) suggests that non-verbal messages expressed through eye contact are very powerful. He adds, "The eyes have a language of their own" (p. 264). When the languages of touch and eye contact are combined, messages that might otherwise be conveyed very awkwardly in words are exchanged instantly and emphatically.

As Montagu (1986) explains, "There is something about eye-contact that is almost palpable" (p. 264), and when it is combined with touch there seems to be a synergistic effect resulting in a potent communication medium. Because of the intensity created in the combination, touch and silence were used together discriminately by the nurses being observed, with some caution and with respect. Usually these moments were short. They often occurred in emotionally charged situations where people either did not know what to say, or wanted to say more than words would seem to allow. This is an example of such a moment witnessed:

She had been a star, an entertainer, a celebrity. Now breast cancer had robbed her of her dignity and her wish to live. On two occasions she had tried without success to hasten her departure from this world. Moments ago the nurse had discovered in her belongings enough medication to end her life. At the moment of this disclosure, their eyes met and stayed locked as the nurse walked to her and took her hand. For several seconds they maintained this stance, frozen together in time.

Absolute Connection

Entranced in your eyes,
the messages come strongly and swiftly.
As you reach out and touch me,
you complete the circuit.
For a moment we are one,
understanding each other completely.

Types of Touch

It is difficult to label a particular touch as belonging to a single category, although certain touches seemed to fulfil specific purposes. A particular touch encounter, however, can achieve a variety of objectives and carry multiple messages. Each touch experience is unique and can be a very private experience between the participants. The stories of the nurses in the study provide insight into the experience from the nurse's perspective, and the observations capture only what could be seen. On occasion, I did ask the nurse to comment on a touch encounter observed in order to provide additional insight.

In the following discussion, the examples of touches observed and recorded in discussion and narrative exchange have been grouped according to their apparent primary purpose. Going beyond the types of touches described in the literature, eight different types of touch were identified through analysis of the study data: procedural touch, non-physical touch, talking touch, trigger touch, social touch, diagnostic touch, comforting touch and the final touch.

Procedural Touch: When a Touch is More Than a Touch

Patients are touched as part of many nursing procedures. However, how a nurse touches a patient during these procedures communicates a great deal about the nurse's feelings for that patient as a person. In this way, a procedural touch may be more than a touch for task-related purposes.

In Bottorff's (1992) study of the uses of touch by oncology nurses, the task-oriented or procedural touch was the one most frequently employed by the nurses she observed. It is the touch that is part of the performance of nursing tasks, such as starting an intravenous line, administering medications, or changing a dressing. If nurses are to accomplish their technical duties, these touches are necessary.

Exemplary nurses did use procedural touches. However, the procedures were performed in such a manner that the touches took on certain qualities. These nurses made therapeutic use of the task-oriented touches, taking the opportunity to perform their work and meet some of the patients' emotional needs simultaneously. For example, when they inspected a subcutaneous needle site, they touched the patient to fulfil this procedure, but they did so gently, without rushing to open the gown to access the location. Their actions communicated their concern and respect for the patient.

Often a procedural touch was accompanied by a secondary touch that was not required to complete the task. A squeeze of the hand, a stroke of the arm or a caress of the face, said, "I care about you." In this way an instrumental and expressive touch were combined.

As they performed interventions, these nurses were able to remain focused on the patients. By providing eye contact and talking to the patient when it was not critical that they be looking at the site of the intervention, they increased the patient's comfort with the situation and sometimes gathered important data. For example, they were able to assess how a patient was tolerating a procedure as it was being done, and then modified their approach if it was causing the patient physiological or psychological distress. If a procedure was potentially embarrassing or painful for the patient, the nurses were careful to maintain emotional contact by touching the patient throughout the process.

One specific procedural touch that was used liberally and effectively by most of the nurses observed was the bath. Jane commented on the importance of bathing patients. She said, "Perhaps it is the symbolic nature of water as the source of life, maybe it is the comfort provided by warmth on sore joints, or it could be the stimulation from water pressure on the skin, but whatever the reasons, nurses love to bath their patients."

Other nurses made comments about their use of bathing as an opportunity to communicate with their patients. They also talked about the tactile stimulations of the bath, the whirlpool jets, the bubbles, the hydrous pressure of the water on the skin. Julie laughed and commented:

We really do wash our patients a lot, probably more than we need to. Let's face it, they don't get really dirty. I think it is a form of therapy. When you combine the stimulation of the water on the skin and the rubbing and scrubbing, it does more than just stimulate their circulation.... It makes them feel much better.

Moria also supported the importance of bathing patients saying, "I give every patient some kind of bath every day. It's a great time to talk to the patients.... There is something about that situation...all the barriers are removed with the clothes, and we really talk." Finally, Lana made this observation, "Giving someone a bath is such an intimate time. I can't think of any better way to get to know my patients."

The dressing change is another nursing procedure that involves touching. This account from my notes on a dressing change observed illustrates the combination of procedural touch with secondary touch:

The old dressing is gently removed. As she works she watches the patient's eyes and face to see how he is tolerating the procedure. Carefully, the wound is cleaned, but before applying the antiseptic, she warns the patient the solution may feel cold. The nurse accurately applies a new dressing. As she spreads the tape to hold the gauze in place, she rubs her hand on the skin around the wound site. She asks the patient if it feels all right, and makes necessary minute adjustments. As she leaves the room, she give his hand a squeeze, and winks at him. They exchange a smile.

In another field note, I recorded this observation of a nurse starting an intravenous line:

She enters the patient's room and explains that the doctor has requested that an intravenous be started. In a careful and complete manner she explains the procedure and what the patient can expect. Returning a few minutes later with the equipment, she applies the tourniquet over the patient's pajama sleeve so as not to pinch the skin beneath. Gently, she rubs the patient's skin to increase circulation so she can locate the vein. As she rubs, she looks at and talks to the patient. Before she inserts the needle, she warns the patient that there will be pain. She asks the patient how the needle feels, completes the procedure efficiently, and reassures the patient as she leaves by squeezing her shoulder. The nurse places the call bell within the patient's reach and asks the patient to call if she has any concerns.

These observations demonstrate how the exceptionally competent nurses approached two different nursing procedures. In each situation the dressing is complete and the intravenous is started, but the patient's feelings are respected and simultaneously the patient is comforted and reassured through touch.

Non-Physical Touch

The second type of touch observed was the non-physical touch. In exploring this area, I saw examples that supported Estabrooks' (1987) claim that touch can be more than skin-to-skin contact. Any modality that allows the human presence to be felt is in a way a form of touch. Music, art, literature, intellectual exchange and non-contact physical closeness could all be viewed as variations of touch that might be called non-physical touch.

The exemplary nurses found ways to touch their patients non-physically. One nurse, Peter, was especially skilled at what I called encircling. He would seldom lay a hand on the patient other than to perform procedural touches, but would often have his arm just behind the patient's back or around the patient's shoulders. Although no physical contact was made, I sensed that the feeling of support was present. The following is an excerpt from a letter I wrote to Peter summarizing some of my observations of our time together:

Finally, I was most affected by your gentleness of manner and by the tenderness of your touch. Your hands are so amazing. Even from a distance I could sense an aura of warmth and healing flowing from them. You have no need to physically touch your patients because you have the ability to encircle them with compassion and caring without direct contact. What power! Your patients are very fortunate to have you as their nurse.

My corresponding field note said, "He doesn't touch as much as he is physically close...and looks directly at the patients, staying at eye-contact level. He encircles them with his warmth without direct contact."

Montagu (1986) suggests eye-contact is a variation of non-physical touch. He calls eye contact "touching at a distance" (p. 124). In conversation, Julie echoed this view when she said, "To me touching is critical. It communicates empathy, caring, affection, concern.... All of this is transferred through touches with your hands and touches with your eyes." Levine (1987) describes eye-contact touching as "looking through soft eyes." Soft eyes, he claims, allow you to see with the heart. I believe this is often the way that the nurses I observed looked at their patients.

Soft Eyes

Your eyes throw light at me.

Some of it I store – my source of hope,
some of it I consume – my source of energy,
some of it I reflect – our source of unity.

Talking Touch

What are the messages embedded in touch? Sometimes, when it seemed inappropriate or too difficult to use words, or the right words to communicate a feeling could not be found, touch was used. This type of touch I have labelled talking touch. Bartenieff and Lewis (1980) describe touch as "the authentic voice of feeling" (p. 287). They conclude, "like music, [touch] often utters the things that cannot be spoken. Nothing need be said, for everything is understood" (p. 287).

In some ways, talking touches share similarities with Bottorff's (1992) category of comforting touch. Comforting touches by Bottorff's definition are given for the purpose of calming, soothing, quieting, reassuring or encouraging patients. Although talking touches do meet these goals in part, they also are used to communicate a variety of additional messages. As the following examples illustrate, talking touches can be used to give the patients specific messages and directions, and are a vehicle for the nurses to share their feelings with the patients and family members.

The following field note describes the use of talking touch by one nurse:

As she cared for the patient and the grieving family, she never said, "I really care," but she said it many times non-verbally by her gentle touching of the patient. Her concern with keeping him comfortable in his final hours: hair combed, mouth and lips moist, her willingness to be the someone close by when the family faced the final moment, all told the family what they needed to hear.

Montagu (1986) said, "Touch communicates the feeling of love. Stroke, caress, cradle, comfort...imply involvement, concern, responsibility, tenderness, and awareness of the needs, sensibilities, and vulnerabilities of the other" (p. 216).

A multitude of feelings were communicated through talking touches to the patient and family members in this situation:

The patient is very ill; in fact, terminal. As the wife and daughter pace anxiously in the hallway outside his room, the nurse approaches them and touches each on the arm as if to say, "I see how difficult this is for you." She leads them into the room, and pulls a chair close to each side of the bed, encouraging them to sit with him and hold his hands. From time to time, the nurse gently places her hand on his pulse or touches his extremities, monitoring him closely but unobtrusively. The priest, summoned by the nurse, prays for the patient; as he does, the wife looks questioningly at the nurse. She responds to the non-verbal question of "How much longer?" by placing her arm around the wife's shoulders. The patient dies peacefully. The nurse beckons the family to follow her down the hall to a quiet room where they can sit for a while. She stays with them, sitting close by and touching them often as they cry.

In talking with the nurse Marie about this moment, she said, "Sometimes those little touches just let the patient or family member know that I am there for them. What I am meaning to say is 'I'm available to you in this time of need.'" Some exemplary nurses indicated they use touch to communicate to patients that they are important to them. Jane commented, "If I think about why I do what I do...I always use a person's name, stand close, look at them, and touch them lightly on the hand or forearm as I speak. To me, this tells them that I am not too busy for them and that I do care."

Touch was used to talk to the patients when the news was too sad or difficult to be put into words. Julie remarked, "When the patient has just heard some really terrible report from the doctor, there is absolutely nothing to say that will match the intensity of the emotion." Lana agreed, saying, "Bad news can only be met with touch. Putting it into words and talking about it right away make it too real. Nobody can bear it, not the patient or me. At times like that I just hold them."

No Match

Stumbling over my tongue,
words are a feeble match for the
relentless pounding of grief.

Trigger Touch

Her husband was only 30, dying a slow painful death from stomach cancer. She was so strong, sitting by his bed all day, sleeping by his side at night, eating all of her meals next to him. The days stretched into weeks and still she stoically sat, asking the nurses and doctors for very little as she met most of her husband's physical and emotional needs.

I wondered about her pain and I worried about her.... I sought an opportunity to get inside, and finally one day it came.

His supper tray was late, and she was pacing the halls awaiting its arrival. Her forehead was riveted with strain and anger. I approached her slowly, silently, and when we were close in physical distance I touched her elbow and said, "It looks to me like you are sitting on the edge of tears. Can you share them?" In a great guttural cry the weeks of frustration and anguish poured freely.

This story provides an example of a trigger touch, a touch that elicits the release of pent-up emotion in the person touched. One nurse, Moria, observed, "Anger, sadness, or despair may come rushing out as a hand laid on a shoulder or a hug says, 'I'm here for you, I care about you, you can trust me with yourself.'" Watson (1989) supports this observation, saying touch may release a person from self-absorption or suffering.

In conversation Mindy told me that she watches for critical talking moments, times when a patient or family member who has been under stress "looks ready to let it go." She said, "Most times it's a little touch combined with a few words that give them permission not to hold it in any longer."

I observed Mindy utilizing this approach. The wife of a man whose condition had been deteriorating daily was sitting outside her husband's room reading. Approaching the woman, Mindy knelt before her and taking her hand said, "You must be tired?" With that small gesture, the words, worries and tears that had been stored up for many days came out without hesitation.

In analyzing her approach Mindy said, "It is a risk every time you do something like this. You might get rejected, verbally or non-verbally, but usually they really want to talk, they just need to be given the chance. You also have to be prepared to deal with whatever you uncover."

Just One Touch

Just one spark,
can start the forest burning.
One rock removed,
begins the avalanche.

A single touch
can prompt a stampede of emotion,
the strength of which
could make any iron man shiver and shake
and beg for mercy.

> But don't be afraid.
> Unlike the fire and the avalanche
> that bring destruction,
> once the stampede of emotion has past,
> genuine calm can prevail.

Social Touch

Bottorff (1992) and Montagu (1986) identify a form of touch they called social touch. By their definition social touch is human physical contact that fosters social bonds and attachment, and permits individuals to maintain their emotional integrity. Montagu (1986) explains that, "cheek patting, hair patting, and clucking under the chin, in the Western world, are forms of behavior indicating affection and social recognition" (p. 270).

In my observations, many of the playful touches such as pretend punches, taps on the nose or cheek, or toes pulled gently were all touches of a social nature. Such physical contacts were made appropriately during moments that were less emotionally intense or to diffuse a difficult situation.

Some social touches seemed to convey a sense of friendliness and playfulness between the two people involved. For example, I observed one nurse trying to get a response from a patient who, although he was physically quite well, had been lying in bed, staring at the ceiling and refusing to interact with anyone since his admission two days earlier. In my field notes I wrote:

> *Every time we enter the room she places her face very close to his, takes his large hand firmly in hers, and talks to him in a playful, yet respectful voice. On one occasion she touches his hand to her nose in a sprightly affectionate gesture...and there it is, a tiny upward crease forming at the edge of his mouth. She has a reaction.*

Jane habitually pinched her patient's big toe as she entered or left the room. When I asked her about it she said, "I just do it to sort of lighten things up.... It's like a bit of fun in a rather serious place. I hope it relaxes them and lets them know it's still OK to play."

At other times nurses used modifications of more conventional social touch, such as the handshake, to signify official acquaintance. Although a formal shaking of the hands was seldom observed, Maureen described how she introduces herself to patients:

When I introduce myself I go up and tell them my name and touch their hand lightly. It's like a handshake, only more. It formalizes our meeting for the first time, but it allows me to find out about them. Do they like to be touched for example, or are they very apprehensive about being here?

In this way the social touch serves more purposes for these nurses than the traditional recognition of the other. It is in some ways also a first assessment of the patient's needs, and a communication to the patient that the nurse is willing to engage in mutual touching.

Diagnostic Touch

Nurses may "identify through touch...body heat, discern skin textures, and recognize changes, favorable or unfavorable" in the patient's condition (Montagu, 1986, p. 133). Touch that is primarily for such a purpose I have called diagnostic touch.

The nurses observed used their hands to assess the patient. For them touch was an important means of discriminating diagnosis. Several nurses talked about this important function of touch:

Feeling my patient's skin tells me a lot.... I touch them to see if they're cold, sweating, dry or feverish.

I read my patient's status with my hands.

I have tested myself – I can tell a patient's temperature with almost perfect accuracy without using a thermometer.

I couldn't start an IV if I couldn't see the veins with my fingers.

How did they develop such an acute and accurate sense of touch? The consensus among nurses with whom I discussed this was that they learned through experience. Lana said, "When I first started I didn't know what hot was. Now that I have felt thousands of foreheads I compare what I feel to what I know normal feels like." As the comments cited imply, diagnosis of a patient's physical status often comes to the exceptionally competent nurses through their sense of touch.

Comforting Touch

Touching was a means used by these nurses to comfort their patients. Morse (1983) claims that the two major components of comfort are talking and touching. She explains, "Comfort measures vary according to situation, context, and meaning to each subject" (p. 16). Depending on these factors, the nurse can choose to talk only, talk with a little touching, or touch with little talking. In Morse's (1983) opinion, all three approaches could comfort a patient.

Benner (1984) recommends the use of touch in providing comfort, stating, "Nurses frequently use touch to provide comfort and reach out to a withdrawn, depressed patient. Often, this human warm contact is the only avenue of comfort and communication available" (p. 63). Montagu (1986) agrees and explains that "Taking almost anyone's hand under conditions of stress is likely to exert a soothing effect, and by reducing anxiety it gives both the receiver and the giver a feeling of greater security" (p. 284).

The nurses interviewed were in agreement with these authors. Julie stated, "Our families in this society are so disseminated and alienated, the only way you get them comfort is through the touch of human kindness." Jane commented, "I think that a lot is communicated through touch. You can show concern...and break down a lot of barriers with touch. It affirms the patient as more than an object. It gives them the ultimate gift – comfort."

The use of touch and physical closeness may be important ways to communicate to acutely ill persons that they are important as human beings, yet critically ill patients are seldom touched by their caregivers in nontechnical ways. Barriers created by the mechanical means used to support life inhibit the use of human contact in providing comfort. A situation observed provides an example of how the exemplary nurse worked around these impediments to bring the patient comfort:

The patient is dwarfed by the obtrusiveness of the machines. On both sides of the bed infusion pumps beep out their progress. Multiple bags of red-labelled solutions drip along, keeping time with the mechanical tones. Chest tube suction devices bubble and honk intrusively. Both side-rails are in their upright position; the aim, to keep the patient in; the result, the world is kept out. The nurse walks up to the unresponsive patient and for a minute watches his shallow breathing. Then she reaches past the cumbersome array of machines and rests her hand on his still shoulder. As she leaves, she gently brushes a few strands of hair back off his forehead.

One day on the unit, Julie talked to me about how she uses touch to provide psychological comfort to the newly admitted patient. She said, "When a patient first comes through those doors, no matter how prepared they think they are, they really aren't. I try to establish some connection with them right away. Often it's just as simple as a little touch." Later she told this story:

We had an HIV fellow with Karposi's sarcoma, a new admission. I was going to help him with his meal. I didn't have any gloves on. This was his first supper with us and he was totally coherent and a little anxious. I introduced myself and was giving him some help with his house coat and he said, "You don't have any gloves on, aren't you scared?" I said, "Well, are you going to bite me?" He laughed and said, "No, but in the other hospital that I just came from everyone wore gloves and gowns every time they came into my room." I just explained to him that when I changed his dressings I would wear gloves but that there was no medical reason to now, and I just kept helping him with his clothes.

After telling me this story Julie made additional comments:

I think I really made him feel comfortable, not that I even touched him that much at that moment, but I showed him I was willing to touch him. I don't think he had been touched by human hands that

69

weren't covered in gloves for a long time. Touching him removed huge potential barriers between us and made him feel a lot less anxious.

In making this patient comfortable and comforted, the nurse felt more comfortable herself. Touching is a symbol of caring, a means to share feelings. It has a dual nature; we use it to comfort each other.

In another experience on the unit, I watched a nurse bring physical comfort and restore control to a patient who was struggling to breathe. This is the field note that described the situation:

Even before we entered the room, I could hear the desperate gasps for air. As I laid my eyes on him I could see his struggle. Starved for oxygen, physiologically by his disease and psychologically by his mind, he fought for every breath. I watched as the nurse walked to his side and took his hand. In a very soft and reassuring voice she said to him over and over, "Take it easy, relax, take it slower." Her repetitive words were matched by repetitive stokes of his forearm. She was so calm herself, and as his eyes fixed on hers, together they slowed his breathing down until the desperation left.

The Comfort of a Touch

Soothe, support, strengthen.
You can do it all with
just the perfect touch.

The Final Touch

Sophia was dying. Life had become heavier than death. Her nurse was aware of her reality and visited her room often that day. Most times there was no medical reason for her visits, she would just hold Sophia's hand, stroke her forehead, sometimes she would pull up a chair and sit for a few minutes and read some of the get-well cards that Sophia could no longer see for herself. This seemed to be exactly what Sophia needed. Someone who was willing to be near, to touch her gently.

Many of the exemplary nurses expressed the belief that the sense of touch is one of the last – perhaps the last – sense to leave the dying person. They agreed with Watson (1989) who claims, "Patients who have no apparent verbal capacity can usually feel a gentle touch and understand its message of caring interest" (p. 23). Because of this belief, the exceptional nurses used touch, sometimes exclusively, in communicating with patients during their last days. Maureen phrased it like this:

I believe that when someone is dying they feel touch until the very end. I tell the family that and I encourage them to hold hands and stroke the patient's forehead. I do it too, just to let them know I am still with them.

Another nurse, Julie, said:

I use touch a lot when a patient is dying or has just died because I believe it is extremely important. I have found that the families watch you.... When I go into a room just after a person has died I always talk to the patient and say good bye and I always touch them. It seems to make it OK for the rest of the family to do that. I have had a lot of positive feedback from families about it.

She then went on to tell me this story:

A young man was dying, in a coma and totally non-responsive. I called his Mom and Dad (they lived out of town) and they arrived just in time for their son's dying day. I encouraged them to help me with his care, to touch him and talk to him. I got them chairs and coffee, and checked in on them often. When I cared for him myself, I reminded him of the presence of his family and I tried to set an example for them to follow.

Near the end they were doing really well and I witnessed something I will never forget. His Mom was washing his face, probably just like she had when he was a little boy. For just one short moment he opened his eyes. He hadn't done that for many days. I know he saw her and she saw him. It was a wonderful moment, a last good bye.

When I asked about her approach to caring for patients near death, a third nurse, Lana, simply said, "I never leave a dying patient without a hand to hold." Several nurse researchers agree with this belief that touch is important in the last hours of life. Blondis and Jackson (1982) contend that, "A great many needs of terminal patients will be satisfied non-verbally through empathetic nursing care. The psychological impact of non-verbal communication, especially of touch, on the dying patient cannot be underrated" (p. 161). Watson (1989), agreeing with this point, reports that, "Our first contact with life is through touch as an infant...our first comfort in life comes from touch and usually our last. Through touch we may communicate with comatose, dying patients when words have no way of breaking through" (p. 22).

A story written by Marie illustrates that the use of touch in the final moments is effective even if the nurse is unfamiliar with the patient and family:

> *It was a busy shift. I had been away on holidays for a month and this was my first shift back. The only patients I knew on the ward were the six I was assigned to. It was about 2100 hours and I needed a dressing tray so I was walking quickly towards the clean utility room to get one. The hallways were darkened and as I walked by a patient's room I was grabbed by the arm by a visitor beckoning me, "Nurse, please come," he said. I entered the room of a patient who was taking his last breaths. He ceased breathing and I looked up at the faces surrounding me. "Is he gone?" asked a younger man, presumably his son. "Yes," was all I could think of to say.*
>
> *I felt so inadequate at that moment, I didn't know his name, the family, or the previous circumstances. I stumbled, "I'm so sorry," and sat down with them holding onto a hand and a shoulder. I knew I was needed by my own patients, but this moment demanded every inch of me now. I noticed how peacefully he died so I shared that with the family, and they shared a few memories with me. For those few initial moments we mostly just sat and held hands. It was like they needed a nurse present for this rite of passage. Soon, the patient's nurse arrived and I scurried down the hall realizing I had a dressing to do.*

When I talked to Marie about this situation she offered further insights. She said:

This man was taking his last breaths.... All I could do was bring his family closer and put their hands on him while I supported them. I realized afterwards how quickly we move in and out of people's lives. I did not know their names, but that short interlude was strengthening to me. I was needed and I also received. I think it was touching that allowed us to make an intense connection in a very short time.

The Unknown Patient

You call for a nurse,
and the nurse in me instinctively responds.

You are alone and afraid
in this moment of need.

I don't know you,
yet you are so familiar to me.
I sense your anguish, your uncertainty.

Hand in hand we unite our spirits
and send your loved one on his journey.

Touch and Silence: The Resemblances

Touch and silence have many similarities. Although they need not always be companions, touch seems to be a natural complement to silence. Like the dialogue of silence, mutual touch is a non-verbal form of inter-human communication. Touch shares a further similarity to silence in that both affect the sender and the receiver, the toucher and the touched.

Touch, like silence, can be effective in both emotionally demanding circumstances and during everyday patient encounters. Both touch and silence were used to communicate and receive messages, feelings and emotions that would be difficult to share in any other way. Touch and silence both facilitate the sharing of emotions.

Comparing further, messages sent through silence and touch involve the similarity of instantaneousness. That is, messages embedded in silence and touch are received as they are sent. There is usually no delay. Both participants can send and receive understandings at the same time, making these two modes of communication efficient.

Unspoken messages are embedded in touch and silent exchanges. Messages that may give the patient comfort and humanize the situation. Although silence and touch are often only a part of a nursing intervention, they are components that seem important in exceptional nursing practice.

The Imprint

Your touch.
A gentle brush across my cheek.
How can something so faint,
so soft,
so subtle,
leave such an indelible imprint
on our souls?

CHAPTER FOUR

SHARING THE LIGHTER SIDE OF LIFE

A merry heart doeth good like a medicine;
but a broken spirit drieth the bones.

— Proverbs 17:22

This chapter focuses on the third theme in the trilogy, sharing the lighter side of life. A light-hearted attitude is common among the exemplary nurses. Despite tragic circumstances in their work lives, these nurses deliberately choose most times to see the positive and humorous side of situations. Importantly, they are able to share this orientation to life effectively and appropriately with their colleagues and patients.

The literature refers to this approach in a narrow sense, labelling it the deliberate therapeutic use of humour. Intentional attempts to introduce humour into patient care using comic videos, cartoons, jokes and clowns are recommended by several writers (Pasquali, 1990; Parfitt, 1990; Gaberson, 1991; Erdman, 1991). Although excerpts from the literature are included in this chapter to augment the discussion, this presentation goes well beyond the staged use of humour in nursing care. As Thomas (1983) says, using humour is more than the presence of a nurse who is a stand-up comedian, an entertainer.

This chapter is divided into four principal sections. First, a definition of this light-hearted attitude is provided. Second, four functions of humour, specifically the communication, social, psychological and therapeutic purposes are described and illustrated with examples. Third, different forms of humour: surprise, word play, black, situational and divergent humour are discussed. Finally, a comment regarding the development of a light-hearted attitude is provided.

Poems are incorporated into the text of the chapter. Nurses' words and field notes illustrate the theme. In this chapter the narratives are especially detailed because, as Benner and Wrubel (1989) caution, "Humour is not easily understood out of context.... It is specific to the situation and easily misunderstood" (p. 19).

The Light-Hearted Attitude Defined

Defining an attitude is difficult. In an attempt to describe what is meant by a light-hearted attitude, four topics are addressed in this section. First, the part that humour and laughter play in this orientation is described. Second, to provide a picture of what such an attitude may look like, various qualities that may be components of this attitude are identified and illustrated. It is proposed in the third subsection that the element of choice plays a part in whether a person has a light-hearted approach. Finally, the role that this orientation to life plays when circumstances are tragic is outlined.

Humour and Laughter: A Component of the Attitude

Thomas (1983) contends that defining humour is like "tacking jelly to the wall." Humour is an elusive concept. Originally, the term meant a liquid that flowed within the body controlling one's health and disposition. Physicians attempted to keep people in "good humour." Humour continues to be considered in part as an internal condition, as in one's sense of humour.

Lefcourt and Martin (1986) define humour as a "complex...cognitive and emotional process" (p. 57). Hunt (1993) establishes that humour can be "many things to many people," that it must be interpreted, and that it is "whatever people think is funny" (p. 35).

Baughman (1974) identifies humour as "our sixth sense...as important as any of the other five" (p. 52). He writes:

> *Much more should be said and written about humour for so many think it means no more than the ability to tell a funny story or to respond to one. Actually, a sense of humour refers to a complete philosophy of life. It includes the ability to take it as well as to hand it out. It includes poise, the capacity to bend without breaking, taking life's responsibilities seriously but oneself not too seriously.... Other less*

obvious components of humour are these: the ability to relax, to escape from tension, to get pleasure out of the joys of others, to live unselfishly, laughing with people [p. 52].

This broad definition of humour is congruent with the attitude displayed by nurses in this study. Laughter, however, though often the result of humour, is viewed in the literature as different from humour. Thomas (1983) defines laughter as a bodily response to things that are both humourous and not so. Lefcourt and Martin (1986) suggest it is "a reflex-like physiologic-behavioral response" (p. 58).

Many exceptional nurses commented that laughter does not necessarily follow a humourous incident. As Julie explained, "Sometimes when a situation is really awful all you can do is laugh. We had a family member who giggled as a reaction to tense situations. He just couldn't deal with what was happening. Especially when it wasn't funny he would laugh."

Humour and laughter are a part of sharing the lighter side of life, but this attitude goes further. It is an all-encompassing disposition, an ability to see the lighter side of situations and encounters as they occur. It is a daily, moment-by-moment alertness to the possibility of seeing the funny, the humourous and the laughable – even in the most unhappy and desperate moments. This spirit of lightness served as a lens through which exemplary nurses viewed their worlds, and through which they helped others to see their own worlds differently.

What does it mean to see the lighter side of life? It is a state of mind in which the humourous, the bizarre and the less traumatic are seen in the events of life and responded to in a light-hearted way. A sensitivity to life's lighter side involves a spontaneity, light-heartedness and an ability to play, all of which are needed for humour to occur. As Leacock (1938) said, it is "seeing the fun of the thing."

Qualities of a Light-hearted Attitude

How does one recognize a light-hearted attitude in another person? The nurses I observed and talked to displayed this orientation to life in a variety of ways. Part of it was non-verbal. Their physical appearance, the way they dressed, moved and used gestures signalled that they were positive, energetic people, open to sharing their vitality. These descriptions of some of the nurses from my field notes illustrate this attitude:

She is bubbly, full of energy and lustrous smiles. Today she is wearing a bright peach uniform, and a name tag that is far from ordinary.

This morning she greeted me with a big genuine smile. The multi-colored smock that she wore over her whiter-than-white uniform made me notice her.

Her arms move in time with her words, her steps are never hesitant. She is open, uses direct eye contact, laughs easily, and proclaims, "I can't be phony."

His approach is playful and full of fun...yet very respectful. Looking into his eyes you see life.

She smiles a lot. I am at once attracted by her energy and vitality. She is someone I want to be around. It's hard to put into words, but she is somewhat like a magnet, attracting me, pulling me to her.

A second part of their positive view of life was shared through the verbal components of their nursing care. The delivery of their comments, including the timing of presentation, was important in communicating this attitude. In one field note I wrote, "The quality of her voice, the cadence and rhythm of her speech, all communicate this sense of zest for life."

One nurse, Peter, was especially effective at incorporating playful comments into his patient care activities. As he was helping a patient put on his pants without success, he would say, "Maybe we should try to get one leg in each hole." While handing out menus on which the patients would mark their meal choices, he would smile and remark, "Here's your homework for today." These little side-comments and the buoyant way they were delivered always made the patients smile.

Choosing to See Humour in Difficult Situations

Looking on the bright side of life is a conscious decision that in time becomes a habit. One nurse, Julie, modelled this belief. She felt that every person has a choice about how they view the events of life. One story she wrote ended this way: "Every day is a mixture of good and bad. No day is 100 per cent good or bad. But you will have good or bad days depending of your focus." When I asked her about the origin of this attitude she told me about a statue that she had seen in New York City. It was a cage, and inside was a pregnant woman with several children clinging to her skirts. The caption read, "We build our own cages." Julie went on to elaborate:

We are empowered to make choices and, unfortunately, we get into situations where our horizons are the edges of the ruts that we dig for ourselves. When that happens, we can't see to either side or the light at the end of the tunnel. It takes the fun out of things. If we just realize we have alternatives as to how we see life, we can breathe.

Another nurse, Jane, wrote, "One's perspective makes all the difference in whether or not any experience is transcending, transforming, depressing or devastating to the people involved."

Marie said, "When I was thinking of stories to write for you, I found that many of the most significant made me chuckle." This humour affected the way the nurses perceived and performed their work. The following stories are examples of how the nurses chose to see the humour in unusual patient encounters:

There was this male patient. He was in isolation so no one could go into his room unless it was really necessary. Often, I would just stop by the door of his room to say "Hi" and see how he was doing.

On one visit he mentioned he was cold. I said I would try to get help, but it was unlikely a repair man could go in to fix his radiator. He smiled and said, "Not a problem, I happen to be a repair man myself." I jokingly said, "Do what you can," and left.

The next time I walked by his room, I peaked in and he had the whole radiator panel off. Parts of the radiator were on the floor. I said, "What are you doing?" He answered, "Not a problem, I've got it under control." What could I do? He was so happy, passing the time, his hands were full of grease and he was smiling. So I just said, "That's great, but we won't be paying you." By the time he was discharged it was all cleaned up and until now it has been our secret.

Another nurse, Marie, told this story:

Mrs. Ling really helped me appreciate cultural differences and to see how some cultures clash with the hospital culture in a funny way. I don't know why but Mrs. Ling really liked me. I didn't even speak Mandarin Chinese or anything. To show her appreciation to me, one day when I went into her room she pulled out these long, slimy red ginseng roots. She said, "Is good, you eat it." I took it and smiled and slipped it into my cheek as I stepped out of the room. I didn't eat it. I just kept hoping that she was right, that it was ginseng. When I think of it, even at the time I saw the humour in it. What a funny sight we must have been, this tiny elderly woman giving me this great "gift" and me trying to stuff this "worm" into my cheek without gagging, all the while maintaining a look of sincere gratitude. I just had to do it because I thought it was probably really important to her. She probably loves the stuff and she had it saved for me. It was a symbol of her gratitude. It still makes me laugh when I think of it.

This is another difficult situation Marie described to me as "humourous":

I was calling this "gentleman" patient for seven consecutive days at home. He was on a research protocol and as part of the procedure I had to phone him and find out how he was doing with his medication and what his pain level was. He was just a really coarse sort of guy, you know, he had frayed edges. When I'd call he'd say, "How the hell do you think I am? I'm not taking this damn stuff anymore." When I'd ask about his pain level it would always be 10 out of 10.

One night when I had to call him, I was not at the hospital; I was at the exhibition. The only phone I could find was in the Silver Slipper Saloon. Phoning him was the last thing I wanted to do. When I called, he characteristically said, "Where the hell are you, at a bar or something?" I said, "You are right, I'm at a saloon."

At the time he was shocked, but we laughed about it together even a day later. I heard that he died, but I was happy that I had this wonderful memory of him. It wasn't tender. We were never close and we certainly never touched each other, but maybe I touched him with my "humour," and he did touch me with his.

Finally, this story is of a demanding moment the nurse described as "the kind that really challenges your funny bone":

Sarah was a Native woman from the reserve. She hadn't been to the city many times and now she had to be hospitalized and was totally overwhelmed by the whole thing. She was my patient and she had to go for a diagnostic test. I had to get her ready to go. She didn't know English, and I didn't know Cree, but I did my best to demonstrate what would be happening to her. She finally understood that she had to take her clothes off and go to the procedure wearing just a hospital gown. I just smiled every time I went to her room. She was just a joy to me, no teeth, beaded moccasins, skin of leather.... She had really lived the teepee life.

The vision I have is of me trying to coax this woman onto a stretcher to go for the procedure. Here I am, a white woman, coming into her room, demanding her clothes, trying to give her an injection in her buttocks.... It was just against her whole tradition, her whole culture; it was just too much for her.

In a swift decisive move, Sarah jumped off the stretcher and ran in her moccasin slippers down the hall. Most of the staff were running after her. I was trying to stay calm, saying to myself, "you can handle this," but another part of me was just so tickled by her spunk. I was cheering, "Way to go, Sarah!"

In these and similar situations, the nurses' inclination might have been to react in a negative way, becoming upset or angry. However, the nurses were open to seeing the humour in these incidents. At the moment the event occurred, and later as they recalled the situations, they chose to see the lighter side.

Maintaining the Attitude

When things are going well,
it's easy to keep the rhythm in your step,
the enthusiasm on your face,
and the shine in your eyes.

But when life gets challenging,
ordinary people lose it.

You don't

Appropriateness of Humour in a Tragic Environment

The sage Epictetus says, "Men are disturbed not by the things that happen, but by their opinion of the things that happen." Maltz (1970) agreed, saying, "In the most tragic conditions and adverse environments, being sad and heavy yourself adds to the unhappiness" (p. 90).

If a light-hearted attitude is a method for survival, it is not surprising that humour and laughter were present on the cancer unit. Nurses who work in stressful environments can need to joke and laugh to cope with the seriousness found there. Feelings that are too painful to deal with can be put on hold or eased by humour. Benner and Wrubel (1989) share this view and add, "Humour is used to establish rapport and alter situations of grave seriousness and despair" (p. 19).

In the same vein, McDougall (1963) writes, "Humour was devised so that we would not be overwhelmed by the misfortunes of life. We are inclined to sympathize too much, and we would be devastated if we did not have an antidote. Laughter is that antidote" (p. 135).

If we accept Baughman's (1974) views on humour it makes it understandable why humour is appropriate and important in an oncology setting. Baughman proclaims, "Humour is that soothing and compensating piece of mind which prevents us from being overcome by life's adversities. It can dissipate the fog and make life more enjoyable and far less threatening" (p. 52). Agreeing with this view, Blondis and Jackson (1982) write:

> *Humour can be realistic, reflective, or honest, and some of our best humour comes out of tension, turmoil, and anguish. It can play an important role in helping our patients, our colleagues, and ourselves... Humour is a means of addressing all that is imperfect in the human condition, it provides a feeling of relief [p. 188].*

After one of my first field days, I wrote:

> *I am surprised by the amount of teasing, joking, and laughter here, not just among the nurses, but with the patients too. I just didn't expect it in an environment that has so much potential to be dark and depressing. Somehow humour and laughter decrease the gloom and replace it with a sense of merriment.*

Mindy told me, "There is always laughter on this unit. It's important for all of us. Some patients say hearing the laughter makes it human here."

As I continued to collect data, my first impression was confirmed. Three nurses explained why it is important to their success to see and share the lighter side of life:

> *I enjoy sharing laughter and do it a lot. I'll see a situation and then inject the absurd into it, just to get a laugh. It's especially important here because people can be stressed and depressed. Laughter sets people at ease. It gives them permission to be spontaneous, to be themselves. It tells suffering people that it's OK to smile.*

> *It's normal and natural to laugh.... It's abnormal not to, even in a place like this.*

Laughing is important in our situation because it can be so sad. In my experience, there is a close relationship between tears and laughter.

Intersecting Lines

Looking into the women's face
I could see the lines intersecting,
lines of laughter and lines of despair,
criss-crossing to form a pattern on her skin.

The way they came together so naturally,
it was apparent they had met often before.

Sharing the lighter side of life on a cancer unit requires impeccable sensitivity and tact on the part of the nurse. Julie commented:

We use humour delicately. It requires a careful matching of types of humour with specific patients and situations. I consider it carefully. I think what kind of humour this patient would like, or would they be open to it at all. When you use humour is important too. Timing is critical.

As Hunt (1993) cautions, "Individuals have differences in what they experience as humour. Individuals also have religious preferences, cultural experiences, and unique values that make certain kinds of humour unacceptable" (p. 35). She continues, saying, "Careful nursing assessment [should] be done prior to utilizing humour" (p. 37)... "like any other intervention strategy, there are indications for, limits to, and contraindications for the use of humour" (p. 34). Pasquali (1990) warns that humour is inappropriate when it ignores client humour styles, ridicules, is racist or sarcastic.

Jane observed, "When using humour it is important to determine what is appropriate and what is not. I am very careful when the patient is in pain, suffering, confused or depressed. At these times it might not be helpful to laugh or be playful." Blondis and Jackson (1982) agree and caution, "When using humour, use not only what is comfortable for you, but what is acceptable to the other person" (p. 189). To be effective, humour must to appropriate to the audience and the situation.

In summary, a definition of this approach to life reveals that although humour and laughter are part of a light-hearted attitude, it goes beyond these elements and is more complex and comprehensive in nature. It includes both verbal and non-verbal components, enactment is a deliberate choice, and it can be appropriate in circumstances that are tragic if it is used with sensitivity.

The Value of Sharing Lightness

It appears a light-hearted attitude serves at least four major purposes. Communication is enhanced, a social purpose is achieved, it has psychological value and light-heartedness performs a therapeutic role. Each of these will be described in the following subsections.

Communication Function

"But most of all, we laugh."

– Leacock, 1938

Humour, laughter and a light-hearted attitude were used by nurses to communicate important messages to the patients. Lana said, "When you have this kind of approach to life, where you see the positive in things, you laugh easily and smile a lot; it tells patients you are a person who is willing to share their lives, their troubles, their joys."

This memory is an example of such a message communicated:

Jerry had been diagnosed with acute leukemia for over a year. As with most patients who receive many courses of chemotherapy, we had developed a strong relationship with Jerry and his wife. Jerry was originally from Scotland and spoke with a thick Scottish accent. He referred to all the nurses as "sweetheart," and that was fine with us. His sense of humour was always present and he was quick to share a joke with a receptive person.

Jerry was in remission and was supposed to have a potentially life-saving bone marrow transplant in Toronto. However, his brother, who was expected to be the donor, was found to have incompatible marrow. The transplant, his last hope for a long and healthy life, was cancelled.

This was his first admission since his disappointing trip to Toronto and the nursing staff were unsure of how to approach him. I was no different, and walking down the hall to his room was one of the most difficult walks I have made. I took a deep breath and entered his room. He was the first to acknowledge my presence. "Hi sweetheart," he said. "I'm back."

I looked at him, smiled, and said, "Don't tell me Jerry, the nurses in Toronto didn't laugh at your jokes so you had to come home."

With that Jerry started to laugh. "You're right," he said. "I missed you girls." That was all it took to break the tension. At that point I sat next to him on his bed and listened as he told me of his trip, his disappointment, and his hopes for the future.

Entering Your Experience

Shared laughter
is a conduit into your experience.
It rivets us together,
so for an instant
we understand.

Another nurse, Maureen, said this about laughing with a patient:

I think it signals to the patients that you have time for them, time for more than the nursing procedures I mean. If you joke around with them, it means you value them. They are worthy of your time and attention.

Humour was sometimes used by the nurses studied when the messages to be communicated were very serious and emotionally laden. In these situations, the direct expression would have been uncomfortable for both the nurse and patient. In the following scenario, taken from my field notes, the light-hearted approach was used to communicate information indirectly. Though the meaning was concealed, the patient understood:

It was late at night and a distraught patient rang her bell and asked the nurse I was observing for an anti-anxiety medication. After assessing the situation, the nurse determined that such a medication would not be appropriate in this patient's circumstances because it could hasten death. To communicate this message to the patient the nurse gently said, "Mrs. James, I'm afraid to give you the pill you asked for because it would make you sleep – sleep too long." For a moment there was silence, and then the patient understood this delicately worded message and they both smiled.

Outside the room the nurse, Julie, offered this analysis of the situation:

I believe in always telling patients the truth, but sometimes it's just too brutal to say it outright. What was I supposed to say to her, "If I give you the pill you want, it will probably kill you." I just couldn't put it that way. The joking approach is better, especially when the topic is such a heavy one.

The Mournful Laugh

Sometimes
the topics that are the most
laughable
are those that are so sombre and sad
that ordinary words can't do them justice.

"Laughter," Moria said, "almost always precedes the tears. It somehow opens the gateway, allowing for meaningful communication of the real issues." Moody (1978) puts it this way: "Humour is an important pass key into an environment in which the locks are always changing" (p. 120). Clearly, a light-hearted approach can enhance the communication function.

Social Purpose

Sharing the lighter moments is part of creating a bond between the nurse and patient. As Jane said in an interview:

When you spend time with your patients laughing and joking togeth-
er, it tells them that you want to share something of yourself with
them; and you get to know another part of them too. This makes you
friends in a way. It gives a sense of solidarity.

Blondis and Jackson (1982) support this belief with their contribution
that "Humour helps establish relationships. If we can laugh together, I'm
your friend" (p. 188). Julie commented, "You are acknowledging a person
when you laugh appropriately. You are saying, 'Yes, I understand what you
are saying'."

Julie shared the following story which illustrates the social bonding that
can occur between nurse and patient and the patient's family members
through humour:

I enjoy laughing with my patients, but one of my unforgettable moments
began by being laughed at. The patient was newly admitted. He did not
want to be here; he wanted to die at home. After all, he owned a funer-
al home and he knew about dying. He seemed to have a dozen children.
They really didn't want him here either. Each was dealing with their
guilt and hurt in their own way. The room was always packed with peo-
ple, but it was not necessarily a friendly place to be.

When I walked in, the hostility was acrid, but my name-tag said
nurse and that gave me licence to be there. Besides, the man was def-
initely end-stage and it would have been totally wrong for him to die
without even having his blood pressure recorded! So in a feeble
attempt to give him care, that's what I did – I took his pressure.

As my stethoscope was plugging my ears, I picked up only pieces of a
conversation that was occurring in the room around me. "I don't
think she could walk this far." "Maybe they have visiting hours."
"She's old you know, and so fat."

Having finally found his blood pressure and wanting to make a sig-
nificant contribution to the overheard puzzle pieces, I very innocent-
ly said, "I couldn't help overhearing. If there's anything we can do to

help with the visit we would be glad to. We have wheelchairs. Feel free to borrow one."

Whereupon the room was filled to overflowing with gales of laughter. One fellow even fell weak-kneed into a chair. Tissues that once held tears of sadness were now wiping away drops of hilarity. It turned out the elderly, crippled, maiden aunt that I had envisioned was an old arthritic overweight English bulldog who probably wouldn't have even fit in the wheelchair!

Yes, the dog did visit. In fact, she monopolized the patient's bed, by this time far outweighing her cachexic master. There were many more smiles and yes, many more tears, both happy and sad, but the bond created by the original faux pas remained strong.

Social Climate Change

Laughing together
makes the social climate,
summer or winter,
ideal.

I watched the exemplary nurses use humour and playfulness in their actions and voices to help them build relationships almost instantly with patients. On one occasion, as we entered the room of a new patient carrying a bag of intravenous solution, the nurse said, "Hi, I'm your nurse, the bag lady." The patient and visitors laughed because this well-dressed, poised, carefully groomed woman was obviously not a bag lady. My field note reads, "They laughed together at the absurdity of the comment and as they laughed the tension in the room eased and the door was opened for important serious exchanges."

The literature also suggests that sharing humour helps establish relationships and aids in creating rapport. Julie talked about this when she said:

There is a sense of cohesion that develops when you share inside jokes with someone. I do this with my patients, and also with the other staff members. For example, we have certain abbreviations that we use that no one else knows the meaning of, like FOS and PON. When we say these code words in report it makes us laugh, it makes us a team, special somehow because only we know the meaning.

Both caregivers and patients are initiators of humour, especially for social purposes. Jane told me she gives her patients permission to joke and laugh by her example. She remembered with delight one patient who followed her lead:

He rang his bell and when I asked him how I could help he said, "Well, I just washed my hair and I can't do a thing with it." It was really funny because he only had one or two hairs left, he had lost almost all of his hair from chemotherapy. We both laughed. At that moment I felt very close to him and I am sure he could tell that I cared.

Julie said, "The patients really seem to enjoy the atmosphere around here. They tell us jokes sometimes. The other day one man told me the rankest joke, it was so bad I really didn't understand it..., but it made us laugh."

Baughman (1974) describes humour as a "social lubricant." It eases social situations, and promotes smooth and comfortable social interaction. Humour helps to establish relationships, decrease fears, encourage trust, increase the feeling of friendship and decrease the social distance as it invites others to come close.

In observing embarrassing moments and errors made, I noticed that humour was often used to "lubricate" these situations. For example, one day Mindy discovered that a patient had not been assigned a nurse and had gone through part of the day without care. The nurse who had made the error was remorseful. Instead of becoming angry or agitated, Mindy just said, "I guess God had him this morning." The situation was resolved, no harm had come to the patient, and a lesson was learned, while the light atmosphere was maintained. Kane, Suls and Tedescki (1977) suggest that humour helps resolve potentially disastrous social interactions by trivializing potentially serious incidents and helping one save face.

I observed nurses using humour when carrying out procedures that were potentially embarrassing or humiliating for the patient. In one instance, Julie had just given a very small, fragile, shy man an enema that had been very effective. The patient was uncomfortable with the process until Julie lightened the scene when she exclaimed, "Why Mr. Godfree, I didn't know you weighed that much." On a similar occasion she said to the patient with a smile, "You done good, buddy."

Nurses who exhibit this sense of light-heartedness convey to others a warmth, friendliness and acceptance. This probably affects how others perceive them. It makes them seem real, human and approachable, the kind of people you choose to trust with your problems and feelings.

In the book *It's a Funny Thing, Humour*, Kane, Suls and Tedescki (1977) describe qualities of humour that make it important in effective nurse-patient interaction. Humour allows the nurse to probe, to find out more about the patient's feelings and fears without taking real risk. In this way humour has an unmasking quality. According to these authors, humour moves people toward intimacy; it is an invitation to interact on a more personal level.

Funny Thing About Laughter

When we laugh together,
it somehow shortens the distance between us,
it reduces the space we occupy,
but doesn't make it
any more crowded.

Psychological Value

Baughman (1974) quipped, "Humour is like a diaper change. It doesn't solve any problems permanently... It just makes life a bit more comfortable for awhile" (p. 61).

Moody (1978) said, "Humour itself is one of the good things of life...to dispense laughter to someone would be to increase the quality of this life" (p. 120). Humour animates and provides a change of pace. For these reasons, and others, sharing the lighter side of life offers a psychological value for patients and staff.

Exemplary nurses believe that sharing moments of lightness helps to comfort patients. Both the nurses and the patients commonly exchanged old jokes that had long since ceased being funny. The patients would say, "I suppose you are going to wake me up to give me a sleeping pill," or the nurse would jest, "You must be feeling like a pin cushion," and both the patients and nurses would laugh. There is some comfort in laughing at these tired jokes. It is analogous to putting on well-worn slippers; it just feels good. If one is still laughing at the same routine, this signals that things are fine, that nothing has changed. Perhaps it is important that they are old jokes and thus their familiarity is a comfort.

Light-heartedness can also act as a safety value, a mechanism used to release stress. Baughman (1974) explains how this happens: "Laughter eases aggression, anger, and distress by taking one's mind off the situation at hand by casting a different interpretation of life" (p. 56).

Lana, in describing how laughter eased the tension in a situation she encountered said, "Somehow even a little titter decreases the intensity of the moment, and makes it so we can carry on." This effect of humour was demonstrated by a nurse-patient encounter I witnessed and recorded:

> *I was watching as the nurse was trying to talk a patient into having a bath she was refusing to take. The nurse had used a variety of approaches aimed at persuading the patient that a bath was in her best interest. At the precise moment when the scene could have become uncomfortable for the patient, nurse and visitors, the nurse said, "That's the problem with nurses. If all else fails we wash it." Everyone laughed, the tension eased and the woman consented to the bath.*

During another conversation Julie told me this story about laughter easing tension:

> *Sometimes the responses I get are more expressions of shock from the patients, but it really relieves the tension when you can get a laugh.*

Yesterday I was looking around for some tube sites on this fellow. The records hadn't been updated so I didn't know for sure where on his body the tubes could be found. As I fumbled around peeking inside his pajama tops and bottoms I said, "I think you should put me up for sexual harassment." The patient laughed and I enjoyed it. It put a lightness into the situation. It covered my incompetence and I think – no, I know – it made the patient more comfortable with what I was doing.

A light-hearted attitude also helps to develop an environment that is warm and nurturing, which is a psychological benefit. It also inspires hope. Moria indicated, "I think the patients like it when we laugh with them. I think they believe that if we are still laughing everything is still OK. It is reassuring; it gives them hope." As Lana said, "A sense of playfulness opens up discussion, breaks the cycle of despair and fosters hope, because if you can laugh you are still alive."

Bradford (1964) reports that::

Humour not only brightens, it cleanses the common life... It is always on the side of hope, high hope. It is always on the side of promise. It asserts that the sun still shines, however dismal the weather of the moment, that the morning birds still sing, and what is more, that there is something to sing about [p. 70].

In summary, a light-hearted attitude helps to relieve anxiety and tension. It is a positive outlet for frustration and lightens the heaviness of critical situations. As Jane commented, "When we laugh it lightens the moment, it provides balance and hope." She called her attitude, her "survival kit."

Therapeutic Goals

Humour can be an important part of caring for clients, caring for other nurses and caring for ourselves. On one occasion in the field, the nurse I was observing, Julie, had encountered a novice nurse performing a procedure incorrectly. She had intervened to prevent danger to the patient and in doing so had caused the other nurse some personal embarrassment and distress. Later that shift Julie used humour to re-establish connections with her young colleague. The field note reads:

> *For the second time tonight we come across Janell having trouble with technology. This time she can't get an infusion pump to start. As we approach her, apprehension is apparent. She doesn't want to make another mistake and her anxiety makes her fumble inappropriately with the machine. Julie gently gives guidance saying, "Press A, then B, and it helps if you say the right prayer." Janell follows the directions and the machine starts running. Julie smiles and says, "See, you must have said just the right prayer." They both laugh and a less flustered Janell is able to carry on.*

The Forgiving Laugh

It is hard for you to laugh with me
and still carry your anger.
Your smile tells me in such a clear way
that I have been reinstated,
that I am once again your friend.

On another occasion a nurse came up to Julie, the nurse I was observing, to report an error that she had made. Julie just smiled and said, "That's OK, we try harder than most. But who can we blame? At times like this it is nice to have someone to blame. It must have been the wandering nurse." During that shift the "wandering nurse" became the scapegoat for a variety of problems including noxious odours and misplaced coffee cups.

I asked Julie about this situation in a conversation. She explained:

> *You have to know which things to deal with seriously, and which situations you can let go. That wasn't an error worth making a big deal about...so I made a joke out of it. It made her feel much better, and I know she learned more than she would have if I'd given her the big lecture.*

A light-hearted attitude helps one meet unexpected events in the course of life. It can be a tonic that invigorates and stimulates those who share laughter. The nurses provided examples of this effect of humour and laughter; they argued that it provides refreshment and restoration for them as well as for the patients. Marie said, "Laughter in a room just fills the room with energy." Jane commented, "laughter makes the world less drab somehow, and more human, much more human." Gruner (1978) agrees, saying, "Human societies treasure laughter and whatever can produce it. Without laughter everyday living becomes drab and lifeless; life would seem hardly human at all without it" (p. 1).

In summary, Baughman (1974) explains the therapeutic function of humour in this way: "It creates happiness, fosters friendship, cheers the discouraged, and dissolves tensions. And as a bonus, it frees the mind, oils the squeaks, and enables us to carry on with fewer dark hours" (p. 52).

The Value of A Laugh

Laughter turns on the lights.

It is a defense against
panic,
sorrow,
and darkness.

It helps tide us over
until dawn.

Humour Comes in Many Forms

What is humour? Why do we laugh? There are descriptions of several different forms of humour in the literature. Many were observed during my field work. Word play, use of the humour intrinsic to the situation, surprise, divergent humour, and black or gallows humour were some of the common forms. Each of these is addressed in turn in the sections that follow.

As mentioned earlier, exemplary nurses attempt to match their style of humour to what the patient appreciates. Jane said, "I change my style of humour to suit the person. I just push the buttons until I get a genuine response." In a field note I wrote, "She takes her humour cues from others as to the type of humour that is suitable, and then improvises." Julie explained:

I probably read them quite quickly. It depends, but I usually try it out when I am alone with them rather than when their families are there because the families may be shocked if I am too familiar. The families are tense, especially at the beginning. I usually use humour after the patient has been here for a while.

Surprise Humour

Marie often used surprise in her approach to humour. In this style, surprise, shock or the unexpected are conditions necessary for humour. This story depicts Marie's use of a "surprise" style:

My brand of humour is usually nice and dry, kind of subtle. This patient I am remembering was diagnosed with a head and neck cancer. He had a history of alcohol abuse. He was impossible. I guess I got the short straw at assignment time and he was all mine. He was gruff, rude, verbally abusive...a real gem. What's more, he required trach. care, suctioning and instillations. A perfect nurse-patient bonding activity.

I remember tiptoeing into his room hoping he'd sleep through my evening shift. Hardly. He was waiting for me, in dire need of suctioning, since he probably refused care from the respiratory therapist on days. Using humour was far from my mind at first. There was nothing he was going to find humourous and I knew it. I was very professional with him and I scraped by for two shifts. But, I had seven consecutive evening shifts scheduled and I realized for the sake of patient-nurse continuity he should be mine for all seven evenings.

By the third shift we had become more familiar with each other. I thought I'd try it. When I entered the room, I said, "Oh no, not you again," and rolled my eyes back in my head. I think my approach shocked him. He didn't expect a statement like that from such a "professional" nurse. Soon, he mimicked my actions, rolling his eyes back into his head when I entered his room. By the fifth shift he broke into a smile, and I got a wink of the eye by the sixth. He and I were eager to see each other by my last shift and shared a few jokes. He did in fact request my care in future trach. procedures. Ah, this I count as success!

In another incident where surprise was used, a patient called the nurse, Jane, into his room. When she entered his room his usually bald head was covered in a curly, long, blond women's wig. The patient looked at the nurse and said, "Notice anything different?" The element of shock and surprise caused them to laugh together for a long time.

Finally, Maureen told me a story in which her own shock response to the patient helped to dissipate the patient's :

A patient slipped and fell on the floor. She overheard one of the nurses commenting that it happened at shift change. The patient got upset thinking that because of the timing of the fall – at the change of shift – the nurses might have ignored her there on the floor until report was over and the replacement nurses were on duty.

Well, I went and talked to her and basically for half an hour I just listened to what she had to say and acknowledged that it was upsetting to think she might have been left on the floor. Then we started talking about other things and I leaned over to her and said, "Next time, just make sure you don't fall at shift change!" She just started really laughing. Over the half hour I figured out that she was quite a character and I knew she would respond to that kind of humour.

Word-Play Humour

Jane used word play, rhyming words and lines from songs when providing care. These were a natural additive to her conversations with patients and others. Talking to a patient one day about his diarrhea, she rhymed, "It's just like the musical fruit, down your leg and into your boot." Entering a patient's room to bring him his noon meal she said, "How would you like a bunch of lunch to munch and crunch?" Her poems and quips did not necessarily fit the context precisely, but the lyrical cadence of her voice was playful and reassuring.

Black Humour

Black humour was used often among staff members, usually in places that were isolated from patients and family members. During team conferences, in the medication room and during report, nurses and other careproviders found a release of tension through humour that was dark and bizarre. Maureen explained, "The staff often use black humour, in the med. room especially. We would never, ever share what we talk about in there with the patients." For example, a physician was observed seriously advising the nurse who was caring for a man whose colostomy just would not stop, that he had ordered the same patient two doses of laxative. In another situation Moria advised her teammates in jest that she was going home early today because "all of her patients were in the morgue." In fact, two of the four patients assigned to her care had died that day.

A field note provides a further example of the staff using black humour:

> *A Catholic priest stopped to tell the nurse in charge, whom I was observing, that the patient he had been called to see did not wish to see him because he was Catholic. The nurse, Julie, said with a straight face, "I suppose she just swore at you and told you to take your cross and go home!"*

Black humour serves many social functions. Julie explained, "It helps to build the atmosphere of teamwork, like we are all in this together. It's easier to work with people you laugh with." Jane shared this view, "The black humour relieves stress. We laugh so we don't cry. We laugh so we can cry."

Situational Humour

Situational humour may be rooted in the nurse's or patient's actions or discomforts. The bedpan that spills, the water jug that tips over – these situations that could lead to other negative emotions and consequences are turned into positive experiences by finding the humour in the event. One day as we entered a patient's room with ice water in hand, the nurse, Jane, tripped over a stool on the floor and flung the water jug into the patient's lap. The patient who could have become upset, just smiled a crooked smile and said, "Well at least I'm awake now."

Situational humour humanizes the environment. The nurse and patient involved in such a situation touch each other with humour. Together they help one another cope with the unexpected.

During a conversation Julie said:

> *Most of the time it is just the situation. Usually it is just spontaneous because some things that happen are really funny. Like the other day, one of the doctors wrote an order that said, "Keep trying to get the patient to suck on his balls three times per day." He meant have him use his incentive spirometer machine, but when we read the order we just totally lost it.*

Divergent Humour

Spiegel (1972) describes the divergent approach to humour as "humour arising from disjointed, ill-suited pairing of ideas or situations or presentations of ideas or situations that are divergent from habitual customs" (p. 7). An example of divergent humour is contained in a commonly heard standing joke in the unit, "Around here, two club sodas equals a party."

A field note provides another example of divergent humour:

> *A patient's daughter had made multiple trips back and forth in front of the nursing station, moving in her Mom's personal belongings. Finally, the daughter said to the nurse I was watching, "That's the last load, just a couple of cases of beer to go." Without hesitation, the nurse replied, "Good, let's put it in the fridge."*

Another field note recalls an equally revealing example of divergent humour:

> *Coming down the hallway towards us was a tiny elderly lady. Her gait was so unsteady she was at risk for a fall. Maintaining her calm demeanor, the nurse, Julie, approached the woman and taking her securely by the arm said, "If the police saw you they would arrest you*

*for impaired driving. Let's get you to a wheelchair." They both
laughed at the proposterousness of this innocent, angelic grandmother
being arrested for anything.*

On another occasion, two nurses were discussing possible interventions to
assist a very agitated bedridden patient. After seriously considering several
alternatives without success, Peter lightened the situation by saying, "That
man used to be a carpenter. Can't we give him a wall to knock down or
something?" The image of this very ill man doing something as physical
as hospital renovations was very humourous. The laughter stimulated further productive discussions focused on solving the problem.

Developing the Attitude

Gelazis (1991) contends that, nurses have been taught and socialized to
maintain a serious demeanor while caring for patients. Humour calls for gen-
uineness and the ability to be yourself, to shed some of this indoctrination.

Hunt (1993) claims that humour is a skill and thus can be learned (p. 37).
The nurses in this study agreed that the light-hearted attitude can be developed and practised. Lana said, "Developing a sense of the humourous
begins by learning to laugh at yourself." Jane commented that, "people
who can laugh at themselves will always be amused" and Gelazis (1991)
adds that, "Laughing at oneself has been associated with maturity.... It is a
use of oneself as the primary instrument of healing" (p. 259).

Our sense of humour evolves. As Steven Leacock (1938) the well-known
Canadian humourist observed over half a century ago, "Both the sense of
humour and the expression of it undergoes, in the course of history, an
upward and continuous process" (p. 8). Exemplary nurses are sensitive to
this developmental change. Jane explained, "I can see a real change in
myself and in my attitude over the years of nursing. Things I laugh about
today I would have cried about a few years ago. Now I can see the fun in
things while I see the sadness." This attitude can be built, like a muscle is
developed, with exercise.

Benner and Wrubel (1989) conclude that humour can "reframe a situation; however, effective use of humour requires a deep background of understanding of the situation and at least a modicum of trust and respect" (p. 19). The nurses I observed had these qualities. They understood from their previous experiences how the patient might be feeling, they had developed trusting relationships with their patients, they were respectful of the uniqueness of each individual and each situation, and they had cultivated in themselves a humourous attitude. Consequently, they were able to use humour appropriately and effectively as a nursing intervention.

Adopting a humourous attitude allows us to reassert our invulnerability and refuse to submit to threat or fear. When we laugh at ourselves, we have a healthy perspective and are able to neutralize our shortcomings. By assuring a humourous attitude we open ourselves to the world and extend ourselves to others.

The Trilogy Reviewed

All three of the themes identified – dialogue of silence, mutual touch and sharing the lighter side of life – share things in common. Using these approaches involves both the patient and the nurse. They are interpersonal exchanges that both participants experience. Both parties are affected by the action or the attitude. It is not a matter of one doing to the other; it is a shared experience, doing with one another.

These are, or they enhance, avenues of communication. Messages are sent instantaneously and simultaneously from person to person. They are all means by which nurses enter their patients' worlds and share their experiences.

Silence, touch, and light-heartedness are all qualities and forces that are felt, that cannot be measured. As Leacock (1938) said, "You cannot weight an argument in a balance, measure social forces with a slide rule, or resolve humour with a stethoscope" (p. 8). I believe this is the case for silence and touch as well.

The complexity and universality of each theme is evident. This brief synopsis of observations and analysis cannot capture fully the intricacy of the myriad of approaches to patient care. However, it is possible that these stories, poems and narratives leave us with a greater insight than we previously had.

Finally, they all expose a basic honesty. Through touch, silence and laughter, a part of each person comes into view, no longer hidden from the other. This opening of the spirit of the nurse and patient allows care to be given and care to be received.

The Can Openers

Touch, laughter, silence,
these are can openers
to your spirit.

They pry off the lid
to your soul
and let me peek inside.

CHAPTER FIVE

THE EFFECTS OF EXEMPLARY NURSING CARE

This chapter provides the final component of the multi-dimensional analysis designed to further understanding of exceptionally competent nursing practice. Subsequent analyses are left to the reader, who may review the data provided and filter them through his or her own beliefs, biases, values and experiences.

In keeping with the style established in previous chapters this final synopsis relies heavily on nurses' words and stories, and on a supplementary analysis through poetry.

Connecting

Stepping Into Your World

There are moments when I feel like
I have stepped inside your world.
For just a flash,
I feel your pain,
I know your despair.
I sense what it's like to have cancer
from the inside looking out
at a world of people who are fit and well.

My God – it's so tragic.
My God – it's so unfair.

Clayton, Murray, Horner and Green (1991) define connecting as "the transpersonal experiences and feelings that lead to the sense of connection, attachment or bonding between a nurse and a patient" (p. 155). This connection between nurse and patient is a complex and important part of the phenomenon of exceptional nursing practice. As described by the nurses, it involves several components: recognizing the similarities, seeing the former you and participating in the patient's experience.

Recognizing the Similarities

Maureen told me this story about a connection that occurred very naturally with one patient. This connection developed partially out of mutual recognition of their similarities:

> *Another patient, a young mother of two kids (notice I picked two women, close to my age, with children).... She had a brain tumour. This was a real warm relationship from the beginning. We shared — we were very close. I was overwhelmed sometimes by what she was going through. I remember how grateful I was for her that she had such a supportive husband. I was in awe of how much strength she possessed. Whenever you admire someone you want to be close to them and study them. She wrote me a poem that I got just after she died. She taught me a lot about me, and made a real difference in my life. I may forget her name but I will always remember her and the ways she was like me, and the ways I wanted to be like her.*

You and Me: The Symmetry

As different as cold and hot,
soft and hard,
happy and sad,
you and me.
Yet even where differences are vast,
there are similarities.

We do share...
a desire to be needed,
a desire to be loved,
a desire to be acknowledged,
a desire to be remembered.

Another nurse, Marie, told me this story of a patient with whom she connected though on the surface they seemed very different:

She was 16 years old. I'd been her nurse right from the very first admission day. We'd grown so very close. Unlike me, she was a wife, a mother and now a very sick leukemic. Just too much for her 16 years to handle. To me she was just a young teenage girl in need of her own mom.

She returned from a pass one Sunday and eagerly searched me out to give me a photo of her 12-month-old baby girl, Amy. I remember how proud she was as she showed me the photo and how carefully she wrote on the back and handed it to me. We both smiled and talked about her little one. I listened intently as a non-mother. This would be the last evening we would spend together in such a happy, carefree way.

Years later, after I had my own little girl, I was looking over an old desk calendar. Amy's photo slipped out and I recalled that evening. I now knew the joy of being a mom, the pride of having your own child and I realized that little Amy brought some beautiful rays of sunshine to a young teenage girl's last days.

In Me, You

We recognize ourselves in others.

In you I see me,
my potential as a mother,
as a woman,
and as someone who will someday die.

The only difference between me and you
is that you are probably closer to your death.

This same nurse went on to tell me a story about connecting – finding a common bond – with a patient named Kenny. She said:

I remember Kenny because he called the hospital from his home up north and said he was never coming back to the hospital in the city again. He was a typical teenager, rebelled all the time, didn't do the things he was asked to do, he was non-compliant through and through.

After some coaxing he did come back to see us for a treatment. I was his nurse. The only thing he really liked was fishing and I thought, bingo, I can relate to fishing. I told him I liked to fish too and he said, "You like fishing?" with total disbelief in his voice. I said, "Yah, I can get into it." He tried some lingo on me about hooks and jigs and I passed. Then he said, "I've got something to show you." It was a home video of ice fishing. The whole movie was of a hole in the ice. The odd time he would say, "Did you see that?" Then he would rewind until we both saw the fish. That was our connection. On each visit I'd always start with, "How was the fishing?"

There is always a connection possible. If it isn't going to be with me, maybe another nurse can do it for that patient.

Overlapping Realities

We are different?
We are the same?
We are essentially the same!

Finding that point where we are the same,
makes caring for each other so natural.

Seeing the Former You

The nurses described the ability to envision the patient in their minds as the person they were before they became ill as an important prerequisite to, and part of, connecting. Three of the exceptional nurses made these comments:

When you see that stretcher coming down the hall with a new admission, the patient at first means very little to you. But as you get to know them, look at pictures of them before they were ill, see their personalities and features reflected in their family members, you feel a lot different about them.

Your first contact with a new patient before you get to know them is hard. They are usually bald, jaundiced, thin...not nice looking. And then you go into their room and start talking to them and all that disappears. You see that person as the person they were before. As you find out more about them you see the person inside, you see their spirit, their soul. I'm not sure what to call it...maybe their essence. The average person on the street would be repulsed by their appearance, but the people here who care so much see only their beautiful side.

I always try to picture what the patient was like before they got cancer. I ask questions about what they liked and didn't like, about their hobbies, their work, their family interactions. Knowing these things just helps me give better care.

In a sense, "knowing" the pre-illness person facilitates establishing a nurse-patient connection. Maureen commented, "It's just easier somehow to connect with the patient if you have known them since their initial diagnosis or at least if you see pictures of them from before [they got sick]. Then you have the total picture of that patient." She went on to tell me this story:

The patient in room 18 was a 16-year-old girl with an astrocytoma. I knew she had been admitted many times before and had become a favourite of the staff, although I had never met her. I knocked on her door and entered the room. There in the bed lay a person, it was hard to know the age or even the sex of the body lying there staring at me with wide eyes. Her face was swollen, typical of the cushionoid syndrome that develops with prolonged steroid use. Her hair was sparse and patchy, revealing her scalp. Her facial features drooped and her mouth sagged in one corner. Her body was swollen and her arm movements uncoordinated. There was evidence of anxiety in her eyes as she looked at my unfamiliar face.

I approached her, gently laying my hand on her arm, and said, "My name's Maureen. I will be your nurse tonight." Some incoherent noises came from her mouth as she acknowledged what I was saying. She pointed toward a list with words on it, showing me her name, Maureen. I nodded and said, "I know, your name is Maureen too.

You know, Maureens are the best people. We should have a great time tonight." She grinned and pointed to a picture on her bed stand. The picture was of a beautiful young woman with long brown hair and a gorgeous smile. Maureen watched me, waiting for me to make the connection that this picture was of her.

I looked at her and smiled. "Is this a picture of you?" I asked. Tears filled her eyes as she nodded. Then I realized how important it was to her that I knew who she was before she got sick, and that she was still that person. She taught me something that night that I will never forget.

When I asked Maureen about this story she elaborated on the lesson she received that night by saying, "I learned that to provide the very best care I need to know who that person was before becoming sick and to realize that person and their history is very important to the patient I am now caring for."

Another nurse, Moria, gave me the same message when she said, "You have to see past the smells, cachexia and crumpled, broken misshapen bodies to see the former radiance." One day on the unit when we were caring for a patient who was in such a state, Moria said, "She must have been such a beautiful woman...just look at her skin and her hair."

Inside the Pebble

Every pebble,
no matter how chipped and broken,
potentially contains
a dusting of gold.

Participating in the Patient's Experience

When I asked Mindy how she defined a "good day" she said, "I know I have had a good day when I make the connection with a patient, when I feel comfortable sitting on their bed or giving them a hug,...when I am part of their experience." Many of the nurses' stories describe times when they made this connection with their patients by participating in their experience through sharing their pain, suffering, joy or an intimate moment with them.

The following is one of Marie's examples of such an encounter:

I want to tell you about one of my patients. He was a doctor himself: very ill, very uptight, very much in need of control over his care. I had known him only vaguely in his previous role as a doctor on the unit, and now here he was, my patient. I was called to perform a difficult procedure on him and I remember purposely thinking, how can I handle this, how can I make a connection with him?

Before I brought in all of my materials for the procedure I went in and sat down with him. I told him my name and said, "You probably don't remember me, but I do remember when you were a doctor here." I said that I really remembered him and that he stood out in my mind because he was so personable and that I was impressed by how he had treated the nurses and his patients. I would have never been able to tell him these things except for the situation, at that moment he was in a more vulnerable position than I was. I just said what I felt, that I was really sorry that he had cancer.

That time together was important. It made both of us feel at ease and I was able to do the procedure then without anxiety. When he came back for another treatment a week later he asked for me. I was glad I had taken the time to make that personal bond. He talked to me about his plans, the things he could never do that he wanted to do. Even after he knew that he was going on with his disease and he stopped the treatments he would always stop by and talk to me. I really miss him.

In this example, Marie participated in her patient's experience by spending time with him, and giving of herself. All of these are part of sustaining the nurse-patient connection.

The same nurse went on to share this example of her participation in another patient's experience:

She was young, sweet, soft-spoken. I just wanted to mother her. She had been through so much. She didn't really understand what disease she had, let alone that it was bad. We were like mother and daughter from the beginning. That was the nature of our relationship. With her I would just say, "You have to do this...," "Listen to me...," "Come on, you can do it...." I wouldn't use that approach with any other patients but with her it just really fit.

I feel as if I shared in her experience. I was with her, at least in mind, from the moment she was admitted until her last day. She was my patient, I was her nurse. When she died, so did a part of me.

The Connection

An unseen thread joins our spirits.

As we journey through this time together
we share ourselves with one another.
Things that would never be
appropriate to say to even my
closest friend,
are, with you, not only appropriate,
but necessary.

We both know that time is short.
To leave things unsaid now, is to
leave them unsaid forever.

"I'm Still Important"

The connection between patient and nurse is related to affirming the value of the patient. An underlying focus of the care given by exceptionally competent nurses is an acknowledgement of the patient as an important and worthy individual, as someone who has value. This is a part of the nurse's belief system as the two enter the nurse-patient relationship, it is reflected in the nursing care they give, and it is an effect of their nursing actions and interactions.

It appears that there are at least four principal means by which nurses communicate to patients that they are valued, that they are worthy people. Specifically, nurses help the patient to be remembered, they help the patient to create meaning out of their experience, they treat patients with respect and help them maintain dignity, and they help patients see their possibilities, to find hope.

Helping Patients Feel They Will Be Remembered

Remember Me

When I am gone,
I have only one request,
remember me.

Say my name,
and remember me.
Touch my things,
and remember me.
Recall my smile,
and remember me.

I simply have to be more than dust.
Dust is just dust,
and when the wind blows it scatters
and is forever
lost.

In an interview Julie said:

People can take almost anything, but they can't take being forgotten. Anybody, if they have one wish, they want to be remembered. Every person wants to make some significant contribution. Sometimes it is part of my role to help them with this.

The same nurse wrote this story:

A young mother of a three-year-old was facing her own death. She had brain mets that were interfering with her cognitive and motor ability to complete the many handicraft projects she wanted to finish and bequeath to her child. The disease was progressing quickly; she was overcome more and more with fatigue and confusion. She asked me to finish a counted cross-stitch picture for her, but instead we packaged up the partially finished picture, thread, and all with a note that said, "My dear, dear child...when you want to, please finish this picture and it will be something you can say we did together...my hand will guide you. Love, Mom."

Another nurse, Jane, said, "The patients, especially near the end, just want to be assured they will be remembered. No one can bear the thought that after they are gone, they will disappear and not matter anymore." I asked her how she responds to these concerns and she answered, "Usually I just help them believe that people will remember them. I say, 'Let's talk about the people who will remember you,' and we talk about specific differences they have made in other people's lives."

Lana said, "Sometimes we have to be part of the group that remembers the patient." She talked about the responsibility she feels to remember certain people, especially those who may not have family members who will recall their memory. The nurses told me about gifts, poems and letters they or the nursing unit had received "in memory" of specific patients. They felt it was part of their role to carry on these memories. Maureen, in telling me about a patient who had written her a poem that she had received just after the patient died, said, "I may forget her name, but I will always remember her. It is just part of what I do."

Jane commented, "A part of remembering is recognizing the uniqueness of individuals, because in remembering we recall what made that person special. There isn't a patient that isn't special in some way."

Helping Patients Find Meaning in Their Experience

In an interview Marie stated, "Probably the hardest question I am asked is, 'Why me?' and all patients ask it in their own way, in their own time. What can I say? It's really, really hard." What she was addressing is the role the nurses play in helping their patients create meaning out of their cancer experience.

Frankl (1969) writes about the importance of finding meaning in our experiences. He says:

> *To live is to suffer, to survive is to finding meaning in suffering. If there is a purpose in life at all, there must be a purpose in suffering and dying.... If one succeeds, one will continue to grow in spite of all indignities. He who has a **why** to live can bear with almost any **how** [p. 50].*

It seems from the examples provided by exemplary nurses that they work together with their patients to help them find their "whys." Expert nurses work at helping patients find meaning or, more precisely, they help their patients make sense out of what is happening to them. In a similar vein Burke (1985) writes, "Each person strives to create meaning out of his existence in the world and attempts to gain freedom from crippling fear, anxiety, and guilt" (p. 95).

Some nurses suggested that when confronted with the possibility of death, the urgency of this search is accelerated. Simultaneously, due to the devastating nature of the disease, this quest becomes more difficult. As Lana said, "How can a person be expected to find meaning in suffering and death? How much more difficult can it get?"

Although the nurses acknowledge that it is a difficult task, they recognize their role in helping patients with their search for meaning within the limits of their individual circumstances. Julie told me this story of a man she helped to find meaning in a life that had been devastated by more than cancer.

> *He was a tall, good looking man. At his request, there was a "No Visitors" sign on his door. He drew pictures, he discussed world politics. He didn't cry...he didn't laugh; he watched. He gave single word answers. His patient history report said he was an atheist. He had attempted suicide because he did not wish to put his wife through the excruciating process of slowly watching him die. He was admitted to prevent any subsequent suicide attempts.*

I personally believe that, given enough opportunities, even the hardest rock can be, if not cracked, at least warmed by the sun. Initially, that rock was all I saw, but this man taught me about the "sands of time" and the importance of approaching every situation with caring and honesty, and to never judge.

I am good at making people feel comfortable. I enjoy helping them get rid of a lot of emotional garbage. I knew he needed to have his inner fears affirmed, to come to terms with the grief and the multitude of losses he was encountering. He needed at least to search for answers to the question, "Why?" I recognized his loneliness and his fear. How was I going to let him know I was there to help?

The opportunity finally arrived one evening. He all of a sudden said, "Do you believe in God?" I answered carefully, not wanting to shut the doors. I said, "I really don't know about God per se. But I do believe in angels."

Regardless of my attempt, his part of the conversation quickly changed to the practical matters at hand, like the size of his pyjamas. However, with the passing weeks, we did discuss angels, a little bit about God, grief, anger, hate, and how unfair this was.

He told me a lot about his life. He had been a young family man during the war, an army officer. One day he and his wife went for groceries leaving their two boys at home. While they were gone, their home was bombed. Their home and family were destroyed. As postwar refugees to Canada, his wife bore another son who died shortly after birth. In an attempt to gather some semblance of normality after all this heartache, they adopted an infant. This child was now in his mid-30s and mentally handicapped.

I think of him often. I was fortunate to be with him in his last moments. I held his hand. All I could do was stand there and hope that he was seeing his kids. I prayed, "Please, if there is a God, this man deserves to see his kids."

I don't know if it was just the effects of his drugs or what, but when I said to him as he was dying, "Your sons are there," he squeezed my hand. He really did. He squeezed my hand and died. And I sobbed.

Finding Meaning: The First Step

You listened to me with openness.
Into your willing heart I poured
my fears,
my sadness,
my guilt.

Now that I am free of these chains
there is a chance I may find serenity.

Just by listening to this patient and helping him to relive his stories, Julie set him on the way to being able to find meaning in his experience. Without this opportunity to free oneself of the guilt, and pain of past failures and sorrows, it would be difficult for any patient to think clearly about what part the cancer experience plays in their life. As Levine (1987) said, "When the mind is clear, we can see all the way to the heart" (p. 66) and "when the heart is exposed there are no obstacles in the mind" (p. 77).

Once the "emotional baggage" has been addressed, exemplary nurses explained the important role of a spiritual element in helping their patients create meaning. As Jane said, "Even if you have never really believed in God or some higher power, it crosses your mind when you face your own, or someone else's mortality."

Most of the exemplary nurses described their own well-developed spiritual beliefs. Having faith in the existence and mercy of a higher being was important in their ability to help patients create meaning. For example, Julie told me:

> *If a patient is really struggling with the "Why me?" and "What will happen to me?" questions and they have no faith of their own, I let them cling on to mine until they can find their own. Some of them never do, but I am glad I can help them in this way. I couldn't if I wasn't sure myself, if I hadn't already found my own way.*

Marie said that patients often found meaning in their disease by first considering it part of their destiny – "God's plan for them." As Lana commented, "Once they accept it, they can start to see the glimmer of good in the devastation around their worlds." Another nurse, Jane, said, "Acceptance of their situation lets them get back control so they can make sense of the chaos and disruption the illness can cause."

Soaring to New Heights

Past the bottom there is an end,
your wings will find their strength once more,
flight again will be your friend,
and onward, upward, you shall soar!

Treating Patients with Respect and Helping Them Maintain Dignity

Treating their patients with respect and helping them maintain dignity was another way these exceptional nurses showed their patients they were valued. The respect that these nurses have for their patients prompted their concern for maintenance of patient dignity. In many of the stories told, this concern underlay nurses' choices and actions. Frequently, nurses were patient advocates in an attempt to provide patients with quality of life as they defined it. As the following story illustrates, doing so can facilitate the sustenance of patient dignity:

He was only 19 years old, far, far away from home and desperately in need of a bone marrow transplant. His home was in a small Native community in Northern Canada. He was Native, and this was his first trip outside the area in which he lived. Naturally, I expected that my task would be to support him and prepare him for his trip to Toronto for his transplant. But the more time I spent with Ralph, the more I realized he did not share those plans and hopes. Ralph always amazed me because he was insightful, spiritual and truly at peace with his situation. He was also very alone, frightened and intimidated by the hospital surroundings. A bone marrow transplant would mean more loneliness and a greater separation from his family and home. A transplant at this stage of his lengthy illness provided only limited hope for a prolongation of life.

Ralph confided in me that his only desire was to return home to be with his family, to experience a familiar sunset before he died. I knew in my heart this could be the only choice for him.... Ralph was an inspiration to me. His decision was not popular with his physician who was disturbed by his "giving up," but Ralph never gave up on his decision.

I, along with my colleagues, were resolved that going home was the only correct plan for Ralph. We presented Ralph's position to the doctors, and defended it adamantly. The bone marrow transplant was cancelled.

Ralph never did return home, but died in room 72 surrounded by his mother, brothers and sisters. He was at peace, and so was I. I truly missed him for some time after. The medical goals of cure and treatment may often be less important when we can clearly distinguish between quality and quantity of life.

Linking Respect and Dignity

Your body,
your right
to decide
its future.

My role,
respect that right
and help you
maintain your dignity.

Patient dignity was also maintained through nursing actions that helped the patients to know that they were still important, that their lives still mattered. The following is an excerpt from a letter I wrote to one of the exceptional nurses documenting my observation of her in such a situation.

Dear Moria:

Today I watched in reverence as you cared for your patient. So gently you removed the mountain of bandages that covered what once was his back and buttocks. You respected his privacy by placing a tiny towel over his chest, the only part of his body that didn't need to be exposed during the procedure. I was moved by this symbolic gesture. You respected him, he was more than a patient to you, he was some-one you cared about. The smells when you removed the dressings were so bad. I wanted to turn away, but you showed no sign that it both-ered you at all. In fact, you moved closer, carrying on a cheerful con-versation with him about his life, his work, his grandchildren. In doing these things you maintained the dignity of a man who proba-bly had only a thread of it left.

Privacy in A Very Public Space

Masterful creation
of the illusion of privacy
does wonders to protect the
last remaining grains
of pride and self-respect.

Oftentimes it is just the respectful ways that the nurses carried out their nursing tasks that communicated to the patients that they were important. The following field notes documented some of the little things that the nurses did for the patients that I believe helped the patients to feel valued:

She takes an infinite amount of time with each patient. Mrs. Long asked to have her legs elevated. Moria makes minute adjustments to her leg positions until the patient indicates that the angle and the sup-porting pillows are perfectly positioned. Even after the sign of approval by the patient, Moria waits to make sure everything is satisfactory.

The attention to detail is remarkable. Warming the towels in the drier so they are cozy after a bath, warming the lotion in the microwave, warming the milk at bed time...all of these take time, but the actions seem to help the patients feel important, valued, more worthy. No request is too much for these nurses. In fact, the patients seldom need to ask. The nurses anticipate needs the patients don't even know they have. The patient is ringing her bell every few minutes. When the nurse I am watching answers her call, the patient's complaint is that she can't find her bell. Later she rings again to tell the nurse she doesn't want to be disturbed. Each time the nurse answers the summons with sincere interest and pleasant patience.

Peter said to me, "Helping patients to feel important can be as simple as knocking on their doors before entering their rooms or asking them what time they would like their baths." Another nurse, Marie, concluded:

Making the patient feel like they are the most important person in the world, even if it is just for the moments you are with them, that should be our goal...that has been my goal. Patients are the priority. It's the little things that make a patient feel important, like the way you enter a room. I consciously slow down my pace as I enter. I take time to sit down in the patient's room and really listen to their concerns. I attend to their needs in short order, not waiting to be reminded. If possible, I anticipate their needs before they ask, like offering them an extra pillow or dealing with a red skin area. You just let them know that they still matter. Even if it is just for this moment, you matter.

The nurses I observed continued to show respect and maintain the dignity of their patients even after they were deceased. In a field note I wrote:

As we enter the dead woman's room, the nurse dims the lights, and tiptoes across the floor to draw the curtains. She talks softly to the woman as she prepares her body for the morgue. In a very quiet voice, she bids the woman, her patient, goodbye.

The importance of showing respect and maintaining patient dignity is supported by Benner (1984). She writes, "Almost no intervention will work if the nurse-patient relationship is not based on respect" (p. 209).

Helping Patients Find and Maintain Hope

By helping patients find and maintain hope, the nurses caused them to feel they still mattered. The following untitled anonymous poem posted on the wall of the nursing unit where this study took place, is a concrete symbol of the importance of maintaining hope.

Cancer is so limited....
It cannot cripple love,
corrode faith,
eat away peace,
destroy confidence,
kill friendship,
shut out memories,
silence courage,
invade the soul,
quench the spirit.
The greatest enemy is not the disease,
but despair.

After reading this poem, Jane said, "If the patients see no hope, no possibilities for even their immediate future, they are left with despair. But it is part of my goal to help them see possibilities, and set goals that are attainable."

Another nurse, Julie, described some of the ways she helps patients realize and accept their limited potential without taking away their hope. She said:

First, you have to honest with patients. People can take a "yes" or a "no" very easily as long as you are being straight with them. When someone is lying there dying, nauseated and in pain, the last thing they want to hear is, "It's going to be OK." At that moment, it is not going to be OK, and that moment is a year long.

Cut the crap.

If they say "Am I dying?" you say, "Yes, you are dying." They are so content with that because someone is telling them the truth. You say to them, "I'm not going to lie to you." Lying to patients destroys their hope. It lets them down. If you lie to them and tell them they will be able to do something and then they can't, they won't chance hoping again.

If they say to you, "Will I be able to walk?" and they won't, say, "No...but let's try sitting up in a chair." If they ask you, "Can I go home again?" and they can't, say, "Probably not but let's try a pass for two hours or maybe you can just get out of your room." Just give them something. We don't have the right to destroy their hope. I never promise my patients something I can't deliver.

Seeing Potential

Your body has been cruel to you,
harnessing you,
limiting your possibilities.

I am here to free your shackles
and set your spirit soaring,
just by helping you see your choices.

Hope is a belief that something good lies ahead. It is not denying reality. Realistic hope can help the dying person face reality, while it also gives them strength to go on living. Jane said, "I think giving patients hope is important. I used to think that being cheerful was a way of giving hope, but now I know it is helping them find courage."

Infectious Hope

Hope.

It cannot be taught,
or bought,

but can it be caught?

In this story Maureen described how she used her nursing skills to help her patient maintain hope:

This patient was in a lot of pain. We had given her breakthrough medication but it didn't work and she was crying out. The nurse who was assigned to her was upset and didn't know what to do. She asked me for help so I went into the room and calmly said, "We are going to try something different." I didn't have a plan when I walked in or even when I said we were going to try something different, I just knew we had to give her some hope.

First, I tried visualization...a Hawaiian beach...that didn't work. So I went into muscle relaxation and sure enough it worked, probably because the analgesic had kicked in by then too. But the distractions of trying these alternatives kept her mind off her pain and let her know we were not going to give up on controlling her pain.

Hope is to Life

Hope.

Without it what is life?

Bleak,
onerous,
hopeless?

Hope.

With it what is life?

Lively,
promising,
possible?

In commenting about hope, Lana said:

It is probably the greatest need our patients have. Those without hope just give up and lead a poor quality of life. Those with hope, have power over their disease and live a good life until they die. The only problem is, hope is difficult or maybe impossible to dispense because it is a quality of the spirit.

One of my field notes reads:

It seems strange to write about death and hope in the same sentence, but where would the dying be without hope? Those who can't find it collapse inwardly and die before they are dead. Those who somehow discover or choose hope have the elusive quality of life the nurses I'm watching desire for their patients.

On the importance of hope for the dying patient, McHutchion (1987) writes,

The hope for the miracle of cure becomes hope for a miracle of care. Patients and families believe that when pain and symptoms of the disease and side-effects from treatments and medications are controlled, the patient and family caregiver are freed to live toward a good death [p. 320].

In another journal entry, I recorded an encounter where a dying man was helped to find the strength to continue hoping for the miracle of care:

A physician approached the nurse I was watching and asked her to come to take a look at Mr. Bill Selsby. Entering the room, we find a man lying in bed, silent, and staring at the wall, his eyes fixed. The doctor concludes that the patient is close to death, and that the diagnostic test scheduled for Mr. Selsby that day should be cancelled.

After the physician leaves, the nurse does her own assessment of the patient. She goes close to him and studies him very intensely. Placing her hand on his forehead she says, "Bill, are you sad? Are you sad because today is your birthday?" She stays in this pose for a few minutes, waiting for a response, a signal, a clue from the patient. I see nothing. She sees what she needs to see.

Leaving the room, the nurse walks up to the doctor and says, "I think you are wrong about Mr. Selsby...his eyes are reacting. He is not dying, he is just down and depressed."

During the day as we visit Bill's room he becomes more and more responsive. The nurse talks to him about his life, asking him questions about his children and his birthday wishes. At first he doesn't say much, but eventually he begins to talk.

Just before change of shift, the nurse gathers her colleagues together to help her surprise Bill with a cake. Together they sing the most rousing and sincere happy birthday song I have ever heard. The man who was supposedly taking his last breath cuts the cake and eats a piece with his tea, which the nurse had carefully steeped to his liking and served to him in a china cup.

In a final demonstration of caring, she places a birthday kiss on Bill's forehead, setting an example for the other nurses who follow her lead. As we leave the room and bid Bill a happy evening, I see the sparkle of life that has returned to those eyes. Bill has hope.

Happy Birthday

"Happy birthday to you.
Happy birthday to you."

You sing with enthusiasm.
You sing with warmth.
You sing in unison.

In the lines
between your words
you sing this message...
Bill, you may not have many
more birthdays,
but let's just celebrate

this incredibly important birthday moment,
and the hope that it brings.

Making a Difference

As the patient is affirmed by the nurse's actions and their interactions, the nurse is also affirmed. From the observations and the comments of nurses, this seems to happen in two principal ways. First, nurses come to know that they are making a difference in the lives of their patients or their patients' families. Second, like patients, nurses also find meaning in their experiences.

Human beings need to feel they are important. One way they do this is by helping or adding happiness to other human beings. The exemplary nurses often commented that they found their work rewarding, in part because through their work they were able to make a difference in the lives of others. When asked to elaborate on their feelings about their work, participating nurses made the following comments:

A lot of nursing is doing for others. When I do something for my patient and it is successful, I feel valued. Like what I do is constructive, and I am worthy. It's a great feeling.

I just know that almost every day when I come to work I am going to change somebody's life. It's an awesome power. I take it really seriously. These people with cancer, they are so vulnerable, so needy. I am privileged to be part of their lives at this time when they need me so much. I always feel needed by my patients...and when I can meet their needs it really makes me happy.

The most rewarding for me is taking a patient from a situation where they are in a lot of distress, or confused and cognitively impaired, and doing a few simple measures that help them to be alert so they can talk to their families and be comfortable...it is so satisfying to give them some quality back to their lives.

The rewards are the little things, seeing individuals come back when they have been through a long journey and seeing them triumph. It's a real joy to share that with them. Even if the patient has died, to have the family members come to you and greet you like you were a real special part of their lives is a great feeling. I think of few careers where you can interact with people so closely and feel so helpful to someone, and feel I really make a difference. It is important to me that what I do is worthwhile.

To Be Valued

I am so alone,
my companions likewise.

But, if I can be vital to but one other,
even for a moment,
I increase my own happiness
by at least one hundred fold.

Maureen told me a story about making a difference in a family's life. She said:

This is a story about a young couple. He was diagnosed with colon cancer and he was only 32 years old. He had two children and so did I. He was really withdrawn all the time and the only thing that could get to him was humour, so I used to joke with him and that would get him talking a little. He was in excruciating pain, but he didn't stop doing the things he loved, like driving his tractor... His wife and I really hit it off – we had a lot in common. She would call me about his pain and other things. One day she called. He was really in trouble so we asked her to bring him to the hospital.

When he got here I could see he was near death. He was confused, dehydrated, atrophied. I took his wife aside and talked with her. I told her exactly what I was seeing.... I said that I noticed a big change in him since the last time I saw him.... I didn't have to tell her that he was dying; she already knew. She told me that it was important to him to die at home so I set about arranging things, medications, home care, all the things they needed to make it possible and we sent them home. He died the next day.

It was an extraordinary time for me because I really felt like I made a difference in their lives. They were important to me, not because they taught me a whole lot but because they made a difference in my life too.

Julie wrote a story about feeling as if she made a difference in a patient's life with a very small but authentic gesture of caring:

There's the time I was "out for coffee" (I don't even drink coffee) with the wife of a former patient. Meeting me again was difficult for her as I represented a very sad time in her life. I had shared the approach to and death of her husband. They had obviously shared a special, loving relationship. She wanted to talk with me again, but it was not without a flood of memories. While we drank our coffee she described to me a moment that the three of us had shared, to which she had often returned during her bereavement. This is the moment.

One time on my perpetual medication rounds I entered her husband's room. I found her and her husband both asleep. He was lying on his bed. She had her head on his chest and he had his fingers interlaced in her hair. It was a peaceful and loving sight. I could not interrupt, so I simply wrote them a note on the first scrap of paper I could find, a little yellow sticky. The note said, "Was here, please call when you're awake. You looked so peaceful, just couldn't interrupt. Your Med. Nurse."

Much to my surprise she had kept the note. She pulled it from her purse that day. It was dog-eared and tattered but she still had it! Her husband had a huge funeral. There were probably hundreds of sympathy cards. It had been more than a year ago. She had travelled, she was doing well, but she had saved this little seemingly insignificant yellow sticky note. A reminder to me that, yes, we all may secretly wish for fame and fortune, the big things are so obvious, but it's the little things that really do make a difference. My little thing had made a big difference to her. I felt so good.

When I asked about the most satisfying aspect of her job, Marie told me this story:

Last week a patient's wife came in and wanted to talk to me about her husband's passing. Weeks earlier, when I was his nurse, I felt like I was one of her family, and it was a really rewarding time though there were a lot of difficult moments. Now, after his death, she was

*reaching out to me again. There were many people she could have cho-
sen to reach out to, including family members, but she chose me.*

The display of thank-you cards on the nursing unit is another concrete
acknowledgement of the difference nurses make in patients' lives. During
visits to their homes, some nurses showed me personal cards, tokens, letters and poems they had received from their patients. These were prized
symbols of the difference they had made in the lives of others, stored over
the years, kept with a sense of sacredness. The following are excerpts from
these messages sent to the exceptionally competent nurses:

> *My grand-mother's life ended with dignity and self-respect. By giving
> this gift to her, not only was her death respectable, but her life (to the
> end) was surrounded with love.*

> *What comfort and peace you brought to my Mother. I will never for-
> get you.*

> *Once in a while you meet someone who is really special. You are my
> special angel.*

> *As I think back over all that we have been through together, I realize
> that I couldn't have done it without you. I am eternally grateful.*

The Miracle Circle

Sometimes,
when I think about
the vastness and complexity of the world,
I am overwhelmed.
I feel so unimportant,
so insignificant.

Then,
I meet you,
and with a small gesture, lovingly given,
I make you feel valued.

The result is a miracle...
when you feel important,
so do I.

It's so simple.
It's so profound.

Finding Meaning in the Experience

As the nurses in this study found meaning in their own experiences in caring for cancer patients, they came to feel valued. Like the patients, the nurses struggled to find this meaning. Making a positive difference in the lives of their patients and the patients' families is one of the ways the nurses found meaning. However, they did tell me of other ways this meaning was realized.

The exceptional nurses value continued personal and professional learning. They seek challenges that facilitate this goal and their work provides these challenges. For many nurses, having this opportunity for ongoing enhancement was a part of finding meaning in their work. As Jane said, "Every day I learn something new about cancer, or about caring, or about me." This finding was reflected in other comments:

When I first started here I planned to stay maybe a year, but now it is two years later and I am still here. When I ask myself why, I realize it is because I still have a lot to learn here.

I just can't imagine a job where you know it all...where you could do everything perfectly all the time. This work is so demanding, so challenging, so dynamic that knowing it all would never happen. That's good. That's the way I like it. That's why I stay.

I really enjoy the opportunity to continue to learn. I go to cancer conferences and come back inspired, proud of what I do, and full of new ideas. I read journals and I'm happy to have the chance to try out the new ideas with my patients.

We can still keep on learning. Even if you have learned the lesson once, you still have to be reminded from time to time. That's the beauty of this job. You never, never stop [learning].

Challenge Seekers

You only become greater
if you are first confronted with
not knowing how.

In your wisdom you recognize this,
and seek
and welcome
the obstacle of challenge.

Exceptional nurses recognize that they were not perfect nurses or perfect people; they were not finished their journeys. They suggested that they did not ever expect that they would achieve perfection, although they enjoyed working toward that unattainable possibility. The result was a yearning for continued learning and growth. In a letter to one of the nurses, Peter, I wrote:

> *I am impressed with your interest in continuing to learn, developing your nursing abilities along with your personal qualities and philosophies. One important point that you helped me to bring to light is that exceptionally competent nurses are not perfect. I think most people equate exceptional with infallible, but that isn't true for any of the nurses I observed. What is true is that exceptional nurses are self-aware, they know their own limitations and their strengths and they adjust their practice accordingly. In addition, they have a desire for life-long learning. I believe this may demonstrate a level of maturity that only rare people reach.*

Beyond seeking and overcoming challenges, there were other ways that the nurses studied found meaning in their experience. For example, Jane described how helping patients create meaning from their experiences actually helped her create meaning from her own experience. She said:

> *Working here, I have come to grips with a lot of the heavy issues – you know, life, death, religion, love, family. You have to help the patients with these issues first, but when you do, you can't help also working through the same issues in your own life. It just happens sort of naturally.*

As we discussed it further she began to debate in her mind which comes first. She said:

I'm not sure if you deal with you own issues first to prepare you to help your patients, or if being confronted with their issues forces you to quickly determine what life is all about. Maybe you go back and forth, you do a little work on your own and then you help your patients and then it's back to you. Yes, I think that's it...I work on it with the patients. Confronting their issues with them forces me to face my own circumstances.

In addition, many nurses suggested that they found it necessary to find meaning in their lives outside of work, in order to find meaning in their work. Again, this was a simultaneous process, working on discovering meaning in all parts of their lives at the same time. There was agreement, however, that they found the searches mutually supportive.

Fog Lifted

What a vague idea,
the search for meaning.
Yet, once found,
it becomes crystal clear.

Joint Transcendence: Living the Extraordinary

In writing about transcendence, O'Banion and O'Connell (1970) suggest, "Transcendence changes things, the past, the present, and the future. Once transcendence occurs there is no retreating. It is more than the ordinary" (p. 160). Watson (1989) is more specific in her description of transcendence, placing her discussion within the context of the nurse-patient relationship. She says:

When both care provider and care receiver are co-participants in caring; the release can potentiate self-healing and harmony in both. The release can allow the one who is cared for to be the one who cares, through the reflection of the human condition that in turn nourishes the humanness of the care provider. In such connectedness they are both capable of transcending self, time, and space. Neither stands above the other [p. 132].

In an earlier work, Watson (1985) writes about "transpersonal caring," a situation in which "both the nurse and patient are changed by the actual caring event" (p. 58). She describes this situation as having a "field of its own that is greater than the occasion itself and which allows for the presence of the geist or spirit of both" (p. 58). To expand further, Watson (1985) suggests that when both the patient and the nurse are fully present in the moment there is a feeling of union with the other. In her words, "the event expands the limits of openness and has the ability to expand human capacities" (p. 59).

In some ways, all of the narratives and observations described in this book illustrate a part of this effect of exceptional nursing practice I have called joint transcendence, or what Watson (1985) describes as transpersonal caring. Yet, no one story or moment observed illustrates it completely. O'Banion and O'Connell (1970) describe the difficulty encountered when one attempts to write about transcendence. They conclude that transcendence "is an experience so far beyond the ordinary...how can we speak of it in everyday words? Of course we cannot" (p. 160).

In following their advice, I have decided to use few words to describe this core concept. Instead the poem, "Shared Journey," attempts to distil from the collection of stories and observations what is meant by joint transcendence.

Shared Journey

Together,
nurse and patient
rise above the pain,
suffering,
and despair
of cancer,
and climb to the top of the mountain that
has no summit.

They take turns
carrying one another.
For they know that neither
can make it alone.

In their time together,
they share through touch,
silence,
and light-heartedness.

In their time together,
they learn about themselves,
their needs,
their strengths,
their limitations.
But most important of all
they learn about their similarities.

They both share the common fate
of mortality,
an understanding which makes
the pleasures of life more intense.

They both possess the potential
for knowing joy,
awe,
and wonder.

They both can understand
that though the physical body
may be diseased,
disfigured,
distasteful,
the spiritual body can be healthy,
beautiful,
and whole.

Through the intimacy of their
relationship they discover
they are valued,
they are worthwhile,
that they can,
and do,
make a difference.
Each, in their own way,
creates meaning out of their experience.

As they reach
higher and higher planes
the patient may leave
to take up challenges elsewhere,
while the nurse,
having gained strength
from the journey
is able to carry on.

CHAPTER SIX

LESSONS LEARNED

The insights discussed in this final chapter provide both a summary of the themes described and a reservoir of unanswered questions. These are understandings and queries that take a wider view of the practice of exemplary nurses. The insights are divided into two groups, those that have potential significance for nurses, and insights of possible interest to other human services professionals.

What Nurses Should Know

Exemplary nursing practice is not only more complex than I imagined, it is also more difficult to capture and communicate than I first supposed. However, I did gain some important insights about exemplary nurses and some unexpected supplementary insights were revealed circuitously. Included in the following sections are the insights arising from the study that may have significance for nurse administrators, researchers, educators and clinicians.

Beyond Competent Care

It appears that exceptional nursing practice is more than competent performance of procedures, although these exemplary nurses were skilled practitioners as well. Although the nurses studied performed the same nursing procedures as other nurses, their care seemed superior. They changed dressings, administered medications, bathed and positioned patients, assessed vital signs and served meals as most nurses do, yet the positive effects on them and on their patients were notable. What was it that made their performance of these procedures different?

I suggest that part of the difference between competence and exceptional competence results from the beliefs and values that underlay the nurses' actions. As Wiedenbach (1964) says, a nurse's philosophy regarding the significance of life and the worth of each individual determines the quality of nursing care given.

Competent Versus Exemplary

I bathe my patient with water.
You bathe your patient in warmth.
I feed my patient toast and porridge.
You feed your patient hope.

I deliver to my patients
medications that make them well.
You deliver to your patients
elixirs that make them whole.

Philosophy: A Blueprint for Action

The exemplary nurses' beliefs were like a blueprint for action. Their philosophies of nursing practice gave them direction, and because they held firmly to their beliefs, their philosophies gave them strength to go against the system and act as advocates for their patients when necessary.

Marie's story about her patient Ralph from an earlier chapter plainly illustrates an association between a nurse's strength of belief and her ability to act as an effective patient ally. Her story bears repeating:

He was only 19 years old, far, far away from home and desperately in need of a bone marrow transplant. His home was in a small Native community in Northern Canada. He was Native, and this was his first trip outside the area in which he lived. Naturally, I expected that my task would be to support him and prepare him for his trip to Toronto for his transplant. But the more time I spent with Ralph, the more I realized he did not share those plans and hopes. Ralph always amazed me because he was insightful, spiritual and truly at peace with his situation. He was also very alone, frightened and intimidated by the hospital surroundings. A bone marrow transplant would mean more loneliness and a greater separation from his family and home. A transplant at this stage of his lengthy illness provided only limited hope for a prolongation of life.

Ralph confided in me that his only desire was to return home to be with his family, to experience a familiar sunset before he died. I knew in my heart this could be the only choice for him...Ralph was an inspiration to me. His decision was not popular with his physician who was disturbed by his "giving up," but Ralph never gave up on his decision.

I, along with my colleagues, were resolved that going home was the only choice for Ralph. We presented Ralph's position to the doctors, and defended it adamantly. The bone marrow transplant was cancelled.

Ralph never did return home, but died in room 72 surrounded by his mother, brothers, and sisters. He was at peace, and so was I. I truly missed him for sometime after. The medical goals of cure and treatment may often be less important when we can clearly distinguish between quality and quantity of life.

The most consistent aspects of the philosophies of the exceptional nurses were a belief that life is precious; a respect for the dignity, worth, autonomy and individuality of each human being; an awareness of the value of self-understanding; a commitment to helping each patient attain the highest quality of life possible, with quality being defined by the patient; an acceptance that death is a natural part of life; and a resolve to act according to their philosophies.

Most importantly, their patients were their reasons for being nurses. As these nurses considered each nursing action or interaction they thought about how it would affect the quality of life for that particular patient as that patient defined quality. The belief that the patient is the primary consideration seemed to sustain them in their practice. This stance made it easier for the nurses to make decisions and helped them be more confident in upholding those choices.

Exemplary nurses would often ask themselves or their colleagues, "Is this action in this patient's best interest?" before proceeding with an intervention. For example, a patient being cared for by a nurse I was observing seemed close to death. The patient had been prescribed a laxative pill. This nurse was about to administer the drug when she said to me, "I've decided to withhold the medication. I don't want her last memories to be struggling to swallow this."

There were many examples of the exceptional nurses consciously weighing the patient's needs against the directives of the system. For exemplary nurses their choices became straightforward when their philosophies of nursing were clear.

Yet, the beliefs held by these nurses were not necessarily static. Perhaps the core beliefs were, but generally the nurses' philosophies were being refined over time through their experiences. At any moment these nurses knew what they believed about each aspect of their practice, yet they were open to changing their beliefs as they encountered new experiences.

Making Choices

When you know
what you believe,
choices are no longer
agonizing decisions,
they are readily prescribed
by your beliefs.

The Importance of Self-Awareness

There were some insights revealed regarding self-awareness, both in the role it plays in being or becoming an exceptional practitioner, and in how it is developed. It appears the nurses in this study learned most about themselves from others, including colleagues and patients. These people were a mirror in which they recognized themselves. Through their interactions with others they identified their own limitations, that no one including themselves is perfect, and that interdependence leads to the greatest potential for success. In these ways they discovered both their own uniquenesses and their essential sameness.

In the oncology environment, and possibly in other stressful, urgent contexts, there is potential for developing high levels of self-awareness. Self-awareness was achieved, at least in part, when the nurses turned inward and faced their own existential questions. The oncology environment may be a catalyst for such introspection.

It appears that because exemplary nurses knew themselves, they were prepared to confront the issue of their own mortality – to understand the meaning of death, theirs and others. For them, being prepared to die was to understand what it would mean to cease to exist as the selves they are. The nurse who understands this may be better prepared to give exceptional care to seriously ill people. Introspection and experience seemed to be ways by which the nurses developed this self-awareness.

The exemplary nurses understood why they were nurses. They believed that they had chosen to be nurses, and they deliberately and regularly reconfirmed this choice. They also chose to enjoy their work and to learn from it.

The nurses' actions and behaviours stemmed in part from an intense knowledge of self and acceptance of self. Part of this self-awareness was knowing what they believed about nursing and about patients, but it also included knowledge of their own physical, emotional and spiritual selves, and an awareness and acknowledgement of their own limitations.

The Physical Self

The physical self includes knowing one's body and ensuring physical needs for sleep, exercise and nutrition. In talking about striving for "total wellness" Julie said:

> *I take care of myself.... If you are frustrated trying to meet your own needs how the wonder are you going to meet someone else's needs. If you haven't decided what is important for yourself and what isn't important how are you going to take these fragile family situations and give them any direction or help?*

She went on to describe the part her uniform and her physical appearance play in her success as a nurse:

> *You don't have to wear a label that says you are a nurse when you wear a uniform. I stretch the limit of the uniform.... I have always been a provocative dresser. I do it as a statement of individuality, because I like*

to be identified. If you care enough about yourself to dress well and appropriately, then the patients will feel cared about too. If you go looking like a slob, how can they possibly have confidence in you? If you can't care enough to put your best foot forward then how can you care about your patients? If you can't have your sweater matching your uniform, then you don't care very much...and the more you care about yourself, then the more you are available to care about others.

The Spiritual Self

Most of the nurses provided insights into their beliefs about the spiritual self. In several cases, this sense of self developed as they cared for dying patients, or faced questions about the existence of a greater power, life and death. Some talked about their belief in God, a higher power or angels, and the power of praying for and with their patients. The following story illustrates this well:

The process of dying can take a long, long time. Mr. Paul had been in the last stages for about two weeks. He was a very religious and devout family man. We had shared many memories together, many discussions in the previous months of his illness. I was there when he was initially diagnosed and had come to know his children quite well. His family had been keeping vigil day and night at his bedside. They had been reading to him, praying his very favourite prayers, and leaving him distance as well. He was very at peace with his dying. But, why, why was this taking so long?

It was Tuesday morning. I was not his nurse that day. His nurse met me in the hallway. She felt that soon he would die. His apnea spells were far too long, his extremities cold and mottled. I whisked through the hallway and caught sight of his wife and two daughters. I clutched one hand and one shoulder and whispered, "It's time." I'm not sure if they knew at that time what I was suggesting. I walked them into the room as quickly as possible. I placed one of his hands in his wife's, and the other hand in his daughter's. I nodded and simply stated, "He's going home." Tears flowed as they said goodbye. I cried too. No matter how prepared you are for death the final moments are always hard. I felt very privileged to be present during this time as many of his family were not there yet. His other children had all been called by this time, and they were on their way.

In a short while, all of his children and their respective families arrived and we ushered them into the room. They formed a circle around him, joined hands, and extended their hands to me, inviting me into their family. Together they recited an "Our Father" and prayed for his safe journey.

I can't tell you how very special I felt to be a part of that intimate circle. It was a gift that would give me a great deal of strength in the deaths I would stand by in the days to come.

Reflecting on this story in conversation Marie, the nurse who wrote it, said:

I often pray for my patients now. When they are dying I pray for them out loud, at that moment. It is my way of assuring their safe passage. I truly believe it and I know if they are aware they would understand. Really, it's for me as well as for the patients.

Another story speaks about the power of prayer in her practice:

She was exactly my age. But that's where our similarities ended. She arrived back early from a Sunday pass and we were overlooking the city from the window of her hospital room. It was a hot summer afternoon. She was worried about her only family member, her 10-year-old son. He was so precious and I had come to care for him deeply. I recall he was wise far, far beyond his years and had taken over as caregiver for his Mom.

His Mom had advanced breast cancer, which was extremely rare for someone her age. She had suffered greatly all her youth in a war-torn country. Recently, she had escaped to Canada and here had suffered an abusive marriage. This all preceded her fatal diagnosis. She was very much alone. As I learned more and more about her, I was chilled

141

by her history. As we talked that day, tears streamed from her eyes. She turned to me and asked, "Why, Marie? Why do these things happen? Does no one care about us?"

We were watching people outside enjoying the summer day. I immediately felt trapped inside as she did. Nothing I had been taught made sense right now. I could not answer her. Tears clouded my eyes as my gaze met hers, all I could say was, "I don't know why. I wish I could tell you."

I thought, what a feeble, feeble answer. I paused for a long time sitting with her. Then I opened up and told her that I was a Christian and that the only thing I knew to offer her were my prayers. I exposed myself to a patient like I had never done before. She thanked me and then said, "I am a Buddhist, can I pray for you too?" I said I would be grateful to receive her prayers.

Perhaps there is something more we had in common. We both had a good Sunday evening.

Marie added a postscript during a follow-up conversation. She said, "I was just totally blown away that someone could have such a devastating life. I didn't know how to answer her, so all I could do was pray for her."

Jane in particular talked about becoming comfortable with sharing her spiritual self with her patients. She made the following remarks:

Spiritualness is part of my practice, but it is a very personal part. Sharing your faith is not seen as a professional thing to do, and in nursing we are taught to be professional so I am hesitant to talk about it and admit to you that it is a part of my care. To me it can be the true essence of everything, of life, of death. I do share my own beliefs if they are asking and they are feeling lost. I feel comfortable because I have my own beliefs together. People ask a lot of questions about the end, where they are going...especially if they haven't finished their business yet. But you do have to be careful. Sometimes I just pray to myself.

The Emotional Self

The nurses described what I have labelled emotional self-awareness. They talked about being "open to feeling the emotion of the moment, and being willing to share those feelings appropriately with others." During their careers they had come to know themselves and to be sensitive to their emotions. Lana commented, "I always believed that if I couldn't recognize an emotion in myself like anger or sadness, how would I know it when I saw it in a patient?" Maureen concluded, "You have to know where you are at. If you don't know where you are coming from how can you be available to help others?"

In summary, the importance of self-awareness, including awareness of the physical, spiritual, and emotional self was identified and illustrated by exceptionally competent nurses. This consciousness developed over time through experience and introspection. The development of self-awareness is viewed as a process. Identification of one's limitations and strengths were part of this self-discovery. A common sentiment is reflected in Jane's words. She said, "Working here I have learned so much about cancer, but even more important I have learned so much about myself. This no one can ever take away from me."

On Developing Self-Awareness

Mirror mirror in my friend,
tell me where this all will end?
What a marvelous mystery,
look at you, it's me I see!

The Significance of Experiences with Death

Many of the nurses' stories and my observations were about death, either the moment of death or the nurse's relationship with the dying patient and the patient's family. Although death is not a frequent topic of conversation and debate in society, these exceptionally competent nurses had thought about death and viewed helping a patient to a peaceful, dignified death as an important aspect in providing appropriate and successful nursing care.

Though working with dying patients was described by the nurses as difficult, they did not seem to find this part of their job abhorrent; rather, they found it rewarding.

The nurses studied articulated and demonstrated comfort with the topic of death and dying, yet their experiences with it seemed to make a profound impact on them. From encounters with the dying, the nurses learned lessons that changed the way they provided care to others. These challenging situations changed them both professionally and personally.

Through Death's Valley Toward the Sun

The walk
down the hallway to the dying patient's room –
it seems so long.

The doors
to the dying patient's room –
so difficult to open.

But anyone
who has the strength
to take the walk,
who has the courage
to open those doors,

may discover an extraordinary opportunity
to learn about the things of life
that really matter.

Moments of Growth

Beyond their encounters with the dying, it appears that many of the significant practice moments reported by exemplary nurses involved patients who shared similar circumstances with the nurse such as age, gender or by being parents to young children. Some nurses wrote, about how these experiences related to their own lives. Other memorable, critical nursing moments revolved around times when the nurses made a difference in someone else's life, when they learned something that changed their practice or their view of the world, and when they had an opportunity to share their knowledge with a colleague. During these significant practice moments when they taught others, nurses also reported learning themselves.

As discussed earlier, exceptionally competent nurses were challenge seekers. It seems that many of these moments of growth came when they faced some of their greatest challenges.

Blending Borders

There you are –
female, 32, a mother.

Here I stand –
female, 32, a mother.

By the nature of our similarities,
the borders of our realities blend.
When you hurt,
so do I.

When you cry,
so do I.

When you die,
so does a part of me.

Touch, Silence and Light-Heartedness: The Trilogy

The nursing actions of sharing the lighter side of life, participating in a dialogue of silence, and employing mutual touch are all means by which exceptional nurses communicated with their patients. Sometimes nurses used these methods of communication while they were performing technical nursing interventions. On other occasions these communications were the sole nursing activity of a nurse-patient encounter. By these means, the nurses let their patients know of their concern and respect for them. In a way, through these actions, the nurses communicated their beliefs to their patients.

A characteristic of these three communication modes is that they are all shared experiences, reciprocal in that both people usually need to be involved. Shared communication may be the means by which nurse-patient relationships are transformed into person-to-person relationships. Watson (1989) describes "human-to-human connectedness" and "transpersonal caring," and I believe that touch, silence, and light-heartedness may be ways by which these are achieved.

According to Watson (1989), in such circumstances "each is touched by the human center of the other" (p. 131). I suggest that when these moments occur there is an inter-human connection that leads to affirmation of value and transcendence of both the nurse and the patient. These moments are, as O'Banion and O'Connell (1970) describe, "Human encounters that have a diamond-like quality of brilliance and value and the potential to make one feel uplifted, completely understood, and transformed in some way" (p. 7).

Person to Person

In the beginning,
when I was a new nurse
standing in front of you
with trembling knees and
gleaming shoes and
text-book approaches,
I called you my patient.

Now,
I stand beside you,
I touch you,
I laugh with you,
I stay with you through silence,
and I call you by your name.

Our relationship is no longer
nurse to patient,
it is now
person to person.

Motivation and Satisfaction: A Miracle Circle

The nurses' stories taught us something about how these exemplary caregivers are motivated to continue to provide excellent care. It seems nursing is a positive and rewarding experience for these nurses. They expressed a high regard for their work. The intrinsic rewards they identified included feeling valued, and the opportunity for continued professional learning and personal growth, both of which they desired.

Many of the examples indicated that involvement in patient-nurse interactions within this context satisfied some of the nurses' priority needs. It seems that their actions in cyclic fashion initiated self-fulfilling reactions. As the exemplary nurses met their patients' needs in an exceptional way, they had their own needs fulfilled. Having been fulfilled themselves, the nurses were able – and perhaps even motivated – to continue to provide exceptional care to meet their patients' needs. In this way nurses were both motivated by and found satisfaction in their work. The consequences became the basis for further exceptional care.

The Miracle Circle Continues

My small gesture,
lovingly given,
causes you to feel valued.

When you feel important,
so do I.

Satisfied that I do make a difference,
I am able to continue to care for you
and for others.

Confronting Cancer: A Shared Experience

One of the incidental discoveries was a glimpse at the nature of cancer. The narratives provide an enhanced understanding of what it is like to confront this disease as a patient, a family member and, most clearly, as a nurse.

The stories reveal that cancer can involve intense human suffering and "chronic sorrow" (Eakes, 1993). This disease shows no favoritism; it has the potential to affect anyone at any age or stage of life. No one, it seems, is immune.

Those affected by cancer and those around them are forced to confront their mortality. Part of the oncology experience seems to be grieving for oneself as well as for others. Confronting cancer causes people to lose their illusion of immortality, to recognize their vulnerability, and their lack of control over their health.

Providing care to those with many types of cancer is like fighting a war against death, disfigurement, and psychological and spiritual collapse – yours and the patient's. The nurses studied showed us that to be effective in this contest, nursing care must be complex, individualized and delivered in a highly competent manner. The nurses fight for themselves and their own integrity as they fight for their patients. It is a shared experience.

From the stories we can sense that the oncology milieu is one of intensity and urgency. At any time any one of the players could lose control, so there is a constant checking to see if they are still all within the threshold of normalcy.

Perhaps this ever-present sense of urgency, combined with the emotions that are part of each encounter to a greater or lesser extent, affected the nursing care given by exemplary nurses. Such an environment reduces the "noise" in relationships and shortcuts are taken to establish meaningful inter-human connections quickly.

The oncology environment has the potential to be very stressful. Oncology nurses ride the waves of emotion with their patients. At any given moment a nurse may be simultaneously experiencing the high of a disease in remission with one patient and the low of disease metastasized with another. It takes a very strong, self-aware person to be pulled and tugged in so many ways and to be able to withstand what would otherwise cause emotional and physical strain. Yet, if the nurses are able to stay with the struggle, like the exceptional ones have, they are forged like steel by the forces of emotions and the energy of experience. Rather than becoming hard and immovable, the nurses become stronger, preserved, able more easily to flow with the forces in their environment. As Martin Luther King said, "What doesn't destroy me makes me stronger."

On Being a Cancer Nurse

Every day you fight a battle against
physical, emotional, and spiritual collapse,
yours and your patients.

Each day is infused with an intensity,
a sense of urgency.
Waves of emotion wash over you
as you move from situation to situation.

At first you are never sure if
the next experience might be the big one,
the one that overwhelms you.

Eventually you find that from each
encounter you emerge stronger,
more sure of your abilities,
confident enough to carry on for the next day,
and probably the day after that.

Messages Addressed to All

Some overarching insights emerged from exemplary nurses' stories that may have significance for people who work in human services fields besides nursing. These insights are described below.

Change: An Opportunity for Transcendence

Our lives are constantly changing. With each change come associated challenges that are opportunities for transcendence of self and others. For example, our level of wellness is not static, and with transitions in our states of well-being, new challenges are presented to self, family and caregivers.

These challenges and changes in life, to self and others, are opportunities for transcendence. Perhaps the more serious the challenge or threat, the greater the possibilities for growth.

On the Changes in Life

Change,
a part of your life and mine.

Embrace it.
Use it.
Grow through it.

Touch: More Than Physical Contact

Nurses and some other professionals, by the nature of the technical tasks prescribed by their roles, have implicit permission to physically touch their clients. Other human services personnel do not have this advantage and may even be discouraged from physical contact with their clients, fearing misinterpretation of such gestures.

However, it seems that touch is more than physical contact between individuals. People can touch one another physically, but spiritual, emotional and intellectual touch are also possibilities. Each vocation may find one or more of these types of touch most appropriate to their work. For example, chaplains may communicate through spiritual alignment, psychologists through emotional contact, and teachers may touch their students intellectually through the sharing of information and cognitive challenges. People in human services fields can take advantage of the communication opportunities provided by alternative approaches to touch, letting their clients know of their concern and respect for them.

Interplay of the Minds

When you share your
ideas and understandings with me,
it tells me
that I am important enough
to be trusted with something that is a part of you.

The Complexity of Human Interactions

Another broad understanding supported by this study is that human interaction is complex and sophisticated, different types of interaction, for example verbal and non-verbal, usually occur simultaneously. People act as they react, and react as they act. The inter-personal process appears to be incessant, fluid and non-linear.

Some of the most important elements in human interactions are the seemingly unheard and invisible. Although we do communicate through well-recognized ways such as speech and gestures, we also communicate by laughing with others, touching them and sharing silence with them.

If you touch someone, remain present with them even in silence, and share with them in light-heartedness, you promote a sense of worth in the other. In the larger view this sense of self-worth in individuals may create a sense of worth in the community and, in turn, in society.

Human Interactions

On closer inspection,
our interactions with others
are not as orderly
as I once thought.

Transcendence: A Shared Process

Another important discovery concerns an increased understanding of transcendence. It appears to be a lifelong process. We are continually refined by our experiences, especially our interactions with others, with self, and perhaps with a higher entity. Being open to the promise that relationships offer may help us transcend to the highest level of human potential. We cannot transcend alone. To reach this premier state of being we must be as open to receiving from others as we are open to giving to them.

A Journey Shared

We cannot transcend alone;
it is a shared journey.

As we transcend through our
experiences with others,
we open up the opportunity
for them to come along.

An Extended View of Beauty

What is beauty? Time spent with the exceptional nurses helped me recognize that our dictionary and societal definitions of beauty are very limited. In the field I saw beauty in many things that are not recognized generally as beautiful. As O'Banion and O'Connell (1970) say, "What is more beautiful than a man weeping, [or]...the eyes of someone welcoming death?"

This extended view of beauty was important for the cancer nurses providing care. Once they redefined beauty they saw the core of their patients, past what society labels as repulsive and unattractive. For similar reasons, others who work with people can benefit from an appreciation of beauty in more than its physical elements. The following story written by Jane illustrates this redefinition of beauty:

> *I think the patient I will always remember is a woman named Heather. She was young, only 34, and she had flawless olive skin and waist length, thick, black hair. Heather was one of the most physically beautiful people I had ever cared for. Her recent diagnosis meant that her chemotherapy treatments had only just begun. I was the nurse responsible for administering her chemo. She was being treated with a combination of drugs known to cause hair loss.*
>
> *Heather had just been hospitalized for her second course of chemotherapy. When I asked her how she had been since her last treatment she talked about some nausea and mentioned that her hair was starting*

to fall out. She was noticing many strands on her pillow every morning. As the days went by the hair loss became greater until it got so that she could pull her hair out by handfuls.

The night I remember she rang her bell and asked if I could help remove the remainder of her hair. I did. We sat together on her bed with a green garbage bag between us stuffing it full of her beautiful hair. I was speechless. In fact, I couldn't believe what was happening. I felt so guilty having hair and being well.

When we were finished we tied the bag closed. I looked right into her eyes, took both her hands and said, "Heather, I think you are still beautiful." I cried and she comforted me. We hugged for awhile and I took the bag and walked away.

Beyond Beauty

You are a goddess,
a beauty in body and spirit.
No matter how this disease ravishes you,
a beauty you will always be.

The temporary
and transient beauty
of your face,
your hair,
your body,
pale against the permanent beauty
of your soul.

The Power of Story-Telling

Stories are powerful ways to achieve insight into human interactions, partly because they are a natural means of communication. For me, they were important sources of understanding. An interview, no matter how unstructured, by its very nature imposes some limits on what is said and how it is expressed. Stories are liberating – they free the tellers so they can share what is important to them and so they can analyze their experiences as they go along. Stories are rich with details about how the experience affected the story teller. The following story written by Marie illustrates this well:

Linda was just 19 years old and she had already lost her arm and shoulder to cancer. I was always amazed at how joyful and positive she was and I thought this can't be for real. But it was. I learned Linda had lots of support at home. She was really close to her sister, and she had a strong religious conviction. I cared for her often over a period of about two years. Whenever we would have new patients with the same diagnosis as Linda, and she was around, she would offer to come and help me teach them about their disease. Using herself as a model, she would just whip off her shirt and show them her scars.

Toward the end Linda met me in the hall and told me that her disease had spread and the doctors wanted her to try radiation treatments. I encouraged her to take the therapy; it was all I could do – she was only 19.

But for her, taking the radiation was wrong and she let me know that it was. I was stunned. I just kept shaking my head and saying in disbelief, "You are not going to try?" I felt upset because she wasn't fighting it. The nurse in me wanted to do something for her. I didn't want to lose her. It would have been easier for me to be more palliative with her if she had been in my age group, but she was only a teenager.

When she saw I was falling apart, Linda took me aside, put her arm around me and said, "No, Marie, it has just spread too much. I can't do this any longer. I'm OK. I know I'm going to die, and I am OK with that." I was shattered.

A few weeks later we had a call from the nurses in Linda's community. It's a couple of hours' drive from here. They wanted to learn how to look after her at home so she could be with her family until the end. I asked to be the one to go to the community and teach the nurses what they needed to know. Though I was eight months' pregnant with my first child, I wanted to be the one to do something for her.

About 15 minutes into the teaching session with the nurses, Linda showed up. She wasn't well. She was thin and pale, but she looked at me and said, "Here I am Marie, I wanted to come today and be your model like I've always been."

Then the class was over and she had to go. I wasn't coping very well with the goodbye because I knew it would be our last. Again she nurtured me. I will never forget what she said...she said, "Marie, it's OK, in fact, it's kind of exciting. Here you are going off on a new journey of motherhood and I'm off on a journey of my own. We are both going to be just fine."

I was so preoccupied driving home. It was true. I was off to become a mom and she was off to...I didn't know for sure to where, or to what; but she did.

As well, telling stories may have a cathartic effect and it can be a further method of increasing self-awareness of the teller. It appears that story telling helps the teller as well as the listener understand an experience. This is clearly illustrated in Julie's comments:

I just want to say thanks for helping me open up a part of me I could have shared in no other way but by writing my stories. There was something so liberating about sitting down with a blank page.

What is Exemplary Nursing Practice?

Exceptional nursing practice is more than being technically competent. It is being self-aware and communicating with patients person-to-person through touch, silence and sharing the lighter side of life. These actions involve nurses sharing part of themselves with patients, and allowing patients to share themselves with nurses.

Exemplary nurses have well developed nursing philosophies that become their blueprints for action. Important elements of these philosophies include a reverence for life and respect for the value of each individual. These nurses have become self-aware and have developed their philosophies at least partly through interaction with patients with whom they have identified closely, through teaching others and through experiences with death.

Exemplary nurses seem to be both motivated by their work and to draw satisfaction from it, especially by the opportunity to feel valued for what they do, and by the chance for personal and professional growth. Exceptional nursing practice includes sharing the disease experience with patients, struggling and growing with them, and using unfortunate circumstances as an opportunity for both the nurse and patient to achieve transcendence.

I believe there is power and promise embedded in exemplary nursing care. The stories and poems presented in this book expose the often hidden, yet invaluable contribution made by clinical nurses. The nurses' words illustrate the challenge of living with cancer and of caring for people with this disease.

Of interest to researchers, this discussion has demonstrated a fruitful approach for collecting, recording and reporting research findings. This technique of coupling credible qualitative methods could be of use to researchers in many human services fields.

For the profession of nursing, this work has contributed to the growing body of knowledge that the profession can consider its own. Some of the essential features of exceptional nursing practice have been explored and described.

There are many more insights that could be drawn from these stories and field notes. Probably the most important discoveries will be made by practising clinicians, nurses who read this book and examine the ideas within the context of their own practice. Well done, my colleagues, well done.

As You Journey Through Life

Touch others,
physically, emotionally, intellectually, and spiritually.

Learn to use silence,
it provides a powerful means of communication.

Approach life light-heartedly,
lightness can be shared even in the darkest seasons.

Focus on the potential,
yours and others.

Embrace change,
it is an opportunity for transcendence.

Find work that you enjoy,
that makes you feel valued and challenged.

Study people carefully,
in doing so you will learn much about yourself.

Determine what you know,
and seek chances to teach it to others.

Discover what you believe,
and live it with confidence.

Appreciate others,
and pursue opportunities to contribute to their happiness.

Realize that you are not perfect,
and accept that you probably will never be.

Know your strengths,
and blend these with the strengths of those you meet.

See beauty,
for it is all around in forms not instantly recognizable.

Be as open to receiving as you are to giving,
this is a gift to others as well as to yourself.

Seek challenges,
and enjoy the privilege of learning from them.

Tell your stories,
for they are you.

Share your journey,
you cannot sparkle alone.

REFERENCES

Arcand, R. (1980). *Stress in cancer nursing*. Unpublished Master's thesis, University of Alberta, Edmonton, AB.

Bartenieff, I. and Lewis, D. (1980). *Body movement: Coping with the environment*. N.Y.: Gordon/Breach.

Baughman, M. (1974). *Baughman's handbook of humour in education*. West Nyack, N.Y.: Parker.

Benner, P. (1984). *From novice to expert: Excellence and power in clinical nursing practice*. Melno Park, CA: Addison-Wesley.

Benner, P. and Wrubel, J. (1989). *The primacy of caring: Stress and coping in nursing*. London: Chapman/Hall.

Blondis, M. and Jackson, B. (1982). *Nonverbal communication with patients: Back to the human touch* (2nd ed.). N.Y.: Wiley.

Bottorff, J. (1991a). The lived experience of being comforted by a nurse. *Phenomenology and Pedagogy*, 9, 237-252.

Bottorff, J. (1991b). A methodological review and evaluation of research on nurse-patient touch. In P. Chinn (Ed.), *An anthology of caring*. N.Y.: National League for Nursing.

Bottorff, J. (1992). *Nurse-patient interaction: Observations of touch*. Unpublished doctoral dissertation, University of Alberta, Edmonton, AB.

Bradford, A. (1964). The place of humour in teaching, *Peabody Journal of Education*, 42(2), 67-70.

Burke, M. (1985). The personal and professional journey of James B. MacDonald. *Journal of Curriculum Theorizing*, 6 (3), 84-119.

Caputo, J. (1978). *The mystical element in Heidegger's thought*. Athens: Oberlin.

Clayton, C., Murray, J., Horner, S. and Grene, P. (1991). Connecting: A catalyst for caring. In P. Chinn (Ed.), *An anthology of caring*. N.Y.: National League for Nursing.

Eakes, G. (1993). The emotional impact of living with cancer. *Oncology Nursing Forum*, 20(9), 13-35.

Ellis, C., and Flaherty, M. (1992). *Investigating subjectivity: Research on lived experience*. Newbury Park, CA: Sage.

Erdman, L. (1991). Laughter therapy for patients with cancer. *Oncology Nursing Forum*, 18, 1359-1363.

Estabrooks, C. (1987). *Touching behaviors of ICU nurses*. Unpublished Master's thesis, University of Alberta, Edmonton, AB.

Fagin, C., and Diers, D. (1983). Nursing as metaphor: occasional notes. *New England Journal of Medicine*, 309, 116.

Gaberson, K. (1991). The effect of humourous distraction on preoperative anxiety. *American Operating Room Nurses Journal*, 54, 1258-1263.

Gadow, S. (1984). Touch and technology: Two paradigms of patient care. *Journal of Religion and Health*, 23, 63-69.

Gelazis, R. (1991). Creative strategies for teaching care. In M. Leininger & D. Gaut (Eds.), *Caring: The compassionate healer*. N.Y.: National League for Nursing.

Glaser, B. and Strauss, A. (1968). *Awareness of dying*. Chicago: Aldine.

Green-Hermandez, C. (1991). A phenomenological investigation of caring as a lived experience in nursing. In P. Chinn (Ed.), *An anthology of caring*. N.Y.: National League for Nursing.

Gruner, C. (1978). *Understanding laughter: The workings of wit and humour*. Chicago: Nelson-Hall.

Highfield, M. (1992). Spiritual health of oncology patients. *Cancer Nursing*, 15(1), 1-8.

Hunt, A. (1993). Humour as a nursing intervention. *Cancer Nursing*, 16(1), 34-39.

Kane, T., Suls, J. and Tedescki, J. (1977). Humour as a tool in social interaction. In A. Chapman & H. Foot (Eds.), *It's a funny thing humour*. Oxford: Permagon.

Kagan, C., Evans, J. and Kay, B. (1986). *A manual of interpersonal skills for nurses*. N.Y.: Harper/Row.

Leacock, S. (1938). *Humour and humanity: An introduction to the study of humour*. N.Y.: Henry Holt.

Lefcourt, H. and Martin, R. (1986). *Humour and life stress*. N.Y.: Springer-Verlag.

Levine, S. (1987). *Healing into life and death*. Garden City, N.J.: Doubleday.

Mallison, M. (1987). How can you bear to be a nurse? *American Journal of Nursing*, 87(12), 15-18.

Maltz, S. (1970). *Critical issues for college health: An inquiry into health problems*. Dubuque, IA: Brown.

Marcel, G. (1969). *The philosophy of existence*. Freeport, N.Y.: Books University.

Marshall, J. (1980). Stress among nurses. In C. Copper & J. Marshall (Eds.), *White collar and professional stress*, N.Y.: John Wiley.

McDougall, W. (1963). *An instinct of laughter: An introduction to social psychology*. N.Y.: Barnes/Noble.

McHutchion, E. (1987). *The family perspective on dying at home*. Unpublished doctoral dissertation, University of Alberta, Edmonton, AB.

Moody, R. (1978). *Laugh after laughter: The healing power of humour*. Jacksonville, FL: Headwaters.

Montagu, A. (1986). *Touching: The human significance of skin* (3rd ed.). N.Y.: Harper/Row.

Morse, J. (1983). An ethnoscientific analysis of comfort: A preliminary investigation. *Nursing Papers, 15*(1), 6-19.

Naisbitt, J. (1982). *Megatrends: Ten new directions transforming our lives*. N.Y.: Warner.

New American standard bible, (1976). La Habra, CA: Lockman.

O'Banion, T. and O'Connell, A. (1970). *The shared journey: An introduction to encounter*. Englewood Cliffs, N.J.: Prentice-Hall.

Parfitt, J. (1990). Humourous preoperative teaching. *American Operating Room Nurses Journal, 52*, 114-120.

Pasquali, E. (1990). Learning to laugh: Humour as therapy. *Journal of Psychosocial Nursing, 28*, 31-35.

Peplau, H. (1952). *Interpersonal relations in nursing*. N.Y.: G.P. Putnam.

Sims, S. (1986). Slow stroke back massage for cancer patients. *Nursing Times, 82*(13), 47-50.

Spiegel, K. (1972). Early conceptions of humour: Varieties and issues. In J. Goldstein & P. McGhee (Eds.), *The psychology of humour: Theoretical perspectives*. N.Y.: Academic Press.

Strauss, A. and Corbin, J. (1990). *Basics of qualitative research: Grounded theory procedures and techniques*. Newbury Park, CA: Sage.

Taylor, C. (1991). On the way to teaching as letting learn. *Phenomenology and Pedagogy, 9*, 351-355.

Thomas, J. (1983). *Extending oneself: Humour as a medium in social studies education*. Unpublished Master's thesis, University of Alberta, Edmonton, AB.

Tough, J. (1989). *The psychphysiological effects of back massage in elderly institutionalized patients*. Unpublished Master's thesis, University of Alberta, Edmonton, AB.

van Manen, M. (1990). *Researching lived experience*. London, ON: Althouse.

Watson, J. (1989). Human caring and suffering: A subjective model for health services. In J. Watson & R. Taylor (Eds.), *They shall not hurt: Human suffering and human caring*. Boulder, CO: Colorado Associated University.

Wiedenbach, E. (1964). *Clinical nursing: A helping art*. N.Y.: Springer.

World Almanac (1990). Boston: Houghton Mifflin.

Then the day came
when the risk to remain
tight in a bud
was more painful
than the risk it took
to blossom.
(Anais Nin)